Free Study Tips DVD

In addition to the tips and content in this guide, we have created a FREE DVD with helpful study tips to further assist your exam preparation. **This FREE Study Tips DVD provides you with top-notch tips to conquer your exam and reach your goals.**

Our simple request in exchange for the strategy-packed DVD is that you email us your feedback about our study guide. We would love to hear what you thought about the guide, and we welcome any and all feedback—positive, negative, or neutral. It is our #1 goal to provide you with top quality products and customer service.

To receive your **FREE Study Tips DVD**, email freedvd@apexprep.com. Please put "FREE DVD" in the subject line and put the following in the email:

 a. The name of the study guide you purchased.

 b. Your rating of the study guide on a scale of 1-5, with 5 being the highest score.

 c. Any thoughts or feedback about your study guide.

 d. Your first and last name and your mailing address, so we know where to send your free DVD!

Thank you!

ACT English, Reading, and Writing Prep Book

ACT Reading Prep Book, English Prep Book, and Writing Prep Book & 2 Practice Tests [Includes Detailed Answer Explanations]

APEX Test Prep

Table of Contents

Test Taking Strategies

1. Reading the Whole Question

A popular assumption in Western culture is the idea that we don't have enough time for anything. We speed while driving to work, we want to read an assignment for class as quickly as possible, or we want the line in the supermarket to dwindle faster. However, speeding through such events robs us from being able to thoroughly appreciate and understand what's happening around us. While taking a timed test, the feeling one might have while reading a question is to find the correct answer as quickly as possible. Although pace is important, don't let it deter you from reading the whole question. Test writers know how to subtly change a test question toward the end in various ways, such as adding a negative or changing focus. If the question has a passage, carefully read the whole passage as well before moving on to the questions. This will help you process the information in the passage rather than worrying about the questions you've just read and where to find them. A thorough understanding of the passage or question is an important way for test takers to be able to succeed on an exam.

2. Examining Every Answer Choice

Let's say we're at the market buying apples. The first apple we see on top of the heap may *look* like the best apple, but if we turn it over we can see bruising on the skin. We must examine several apples before deciding which apple is the best. Finding the correct answer choice is like finding the best apple. Although it's tempting to choose an answer that seems correct at first without reading the others, it's important to read each answer choice thoroughly before making a final decision on the answer. The aim of a test writer might be to get as close as possible to the correct answer, so watch out for subtle words that may indicate an answer is incorrect. Once the correct answer choice is selected, read the question again and the answer in response to make sure all your bases are covered.

3. Eliminating Wrong Answer Choices

Sometimes we become paralyzed when we are confronted with too many choices. Which frozen yogurt flavor is the tastiest? Which pair of shoes look the best with this outfit? What type of car will fill my needs as a consumer? If you are unsure of which answer would be the best to choose, it may help to use process of elimination. We use "filtering" all the time on sites such as eBay® or Craigslist® to eliminate the ads that are not right for us. We can do the same thing on an exam. Process of elimination is crossing out the answer choices we know for sure are wrong and leaving the ones that might be correct. It may help to cover up the incorrect answer choice. Covering incorrect choices is a psychological act that alleviates stress due to the brain being exposed to a smaller amount of information. Choosing between two answer choices is much easier than choosing between all of them, and you have a better chance of selecting the correct answer if you have less to focus on.

4. Sticking to the World of the Question

When we are attempting to answer questions, our minds will often wander away from the question and what it is asking. We begin to see answer choices that are true in the real world instead of true in the world of the question. It may be helpful to think of each test question as its own little world. This world may be different from ours. This world may know as a truth that the chicken came before the egg or may assert that two plus two equals five. Remember that, no matter what hypothetical nonsense may be in the question, assume it to be true. If the question states that the chicken came before the egg, then choose your answer based on that truth. Sticking to the world of the question means placing all of our biases and assumptions aside and relying on the question to guide us to the correct answer. If we are simply looking for answers that are correct based on our own judgment, then we may choose incorrectly. Remember an answer that is true does not necessarily answer the question.

5. Key Words

If you come across a complex test question that you have to read over and over again, try pulling out some key words from the question in order to understand what exactly it is asking. Key words may be words that surround the question, such as *main idea, analogous, parallel, resembles, structured,* or *defines*. The question may be asking for the main idea, or it may be asking you to define something. Deconstructing the sentence may also be helpful in making the question simpler before trying to answer it. This means taking the sentence apart and obtaining meaning in pieces, or separating the question from the foundation of the question. For example, let's look at this question:

> Given the author's description of the content of paleontology in the first paragraph, which of the following is most parallel to what it taught?

The question asks which one of the answers most *parallels* the following information: The *description* of paleontology in the first paragraph. The first step would be to see *how* paleontology is described in the first paragraph. Then, we would find an answer choice that parallels that description. The question seems complex at first, but after we deconstruct it, the answer becomes much more attainable.

6. Subtle Negatives

Negative words in question stems will be words such as *not, but, neither,* or *except*. Test writers often use these words in order to trick unsuspecting test takers into selecting the wrong answer—or, at least, to test their reading comprehension of the question. Many exams will feature the negative words in all caps (*which of the following is NOT an example*), but some questions will add the negative word seamlessly into the sentence. The following is an example of a subtle negative used in a question stem:

> According to the passage, which of the following is *not* considered to be an example of paleontology?

If we rush through the exam, we might skip that tiny word, *not,* inside the question, and choose an answer that is opposite of the correct choice. Again, it's important to read the question fully, and double check for any words that may negate the statement in any way.

7. Spotting the Hedges

The word "hedging" refers to language that remains vague or avoids absolute terminology. Absolute terminology consists of words like *always, never, all, every, just, only, none,* and *must*. Hedging refers to words like *seem, tend, might, most, some, sometimes, perhaps, possibly, probability,* and *often*. In some cases, we want to choose answer choices that use hedging and avoid answer choices that use absolute terminology. It's important to pay attention to what subject you are on and adjust your response accordingly.

8. Restating to Understand

Every now and then we come across questions that we don't understand. The language may be too complex, or the question is structured in a way that is meant to confuse the test taker. When you come across a question like this, it may be worth your time to rewrite or restate the question in your own words in order to understand it better. For example, let's look at the following complicated question:

> Which of the following words, if substituted for the word *parochial* in the first paragraph, would LEAST change the meaning of the sentence?

Let's restate the question in order to understand it better. We know that they want the word *parochial* replaced. We also know that this new word would "least" or "not" change the meaning of the sentence. Now let's try the sentence again:

> Which word could we replace with *parochial,* and it would not change the meaning?

Restating it this way, we see that the question is asking for a synonym. Now, let's restate the question so we can answer it better:

> Which word is a synonym for the word *parochial?*

Before we even look at the answer choices, we have a simpler, restated version of a complicated question.

9. Predicting the Answer

After you read the question, try predicting the answer *before* reading the answer choices. By formulating an answer in your mind, you will be less likely to be distracted by any wrong answer choices. Using predictions will also help you feel more confident in the answer choice you select. Once you've chosen your answer, go back and reread the question and answer choices to make sure you have the best fit. If you have no idea what the answer may be for a particular question, forego using this strategy.

10. Avoiding Patterns

One popular myth in grade school relating to standardized testing is that test writers will often put multiple-choice answers in patterns. A runoff example of this kind of thinking is that the most common answer choice is "C," with "B" following close behind. Or, some will advocate certain made-up word patterns that simply do not exist. Test writers do not arrange their correct answer choices in any kind of pattern; their choices are randomized. There may even be times where the correct answer choice will be the same letter for two or three questions in a row, but we have no way of knowing when or if this might happen. Instead of trying to figure out what choice the test writer probably set as being correct, focus on what the *best answer choice* would be out of the answers you are presented with. Use the tips above, general knowledge, and reading comprehension skills in order to best answer the question, rather than looking for patterns that do not exist.

FREE DVD OFFER

Achieving a high score on your exam depends not only on understanding the content, but also on understanding how to apply your knowledge and your command of test taking strategies. **Because your success is our primary goal, we offer a FREE Study Tips DVD, which provides top-notch test taking strategies to help you optimize your testing experience.**

Our simple request in exchange for the strategy-packed DVD is that you email us your feedback about our study guide.

To receive your **FREE Study Tips DVD**, email freedvd@apexprep.com. Please put "FREE DVD" in the subject line and put the following in the email:

    a. The name of the study guide you purchased.

    b. Your rating of the study guide on a scale of 1-5, with 5 being the highest score.

    c. Any thoughts or feedback about your study guide.

    d. Your first and last name and your mailing address, so we know where to send your free DVD!

Introduction to the ACT

Function of the Test

The ACT is one of the two national standardized college entrance examinations, with the SAT serving as the other option. Most hopeful college-bound students take the ACT, SAT, or both. For admissions purposes, every four-year college and university in the United States accepts ACE scores, and some schools require it. More so than the SAT, which primarily serves as an aptitude test, the ACT is often used for course placement purposes because it measures academic achievement on content addressed in high school classes. Twelve states also require that all high school juniors in the state take the ACT, and eight additional states have counties that require the exam.

Most ACT test takers are prospective college students who are currently in their junior or senior year of high school. More than 2 millions students graduating in the class of 2017 took the ACT.

Test Administration

The ACT is offered on seven dates in the U.S. and Canada, and on six dates internationally throughout the year. The exam is usually administered at high schools or colleges, but other locations may be offered. The registration fee includes the cost to submit score reports to four colleges, but for an additional fee, students can send scores to additional institutions. There is a separate registration fee incurred for the optional writing section. Some high schools cover the fees for their students, so prospective test takers are advised to contact the guidance counselor at their school.

Test takers can retake the ACT every time the test is offered, up to a maximum of twelve times. However, different colleges and universities sometimes have limits on the number of retakes they will consider. Moreover, scores from the various test sections cannot be combined from different test attempts. Reasonable accommodations will be provided to test takers with appropriate documentation for a variety of disabilities.

Test Format

Test takers are given a total of 175 minutes to complete the 215 multiple-choice questions in four subject subtests (English, Mathematics, Reading, and Science) of the ACT. It also has an optional Writing Test, which involves writing an essay, which takes an additional forty minutes. Some colleges and universities require the essay for admission.

The English Test consists of 75 questions that address the production of writing, knowledge of language, and conventions of standard English. The 60-question Mathematics Test involves number sense, algebra, functions, geometry, statistics and probability, and modeling. Calculators that meet certain calculator requirements are permitted. The Reading Test is contains four written passages, with ten questions per passage addressing comprehension skills, the ability to make inferences and draw conclusions, and apply and integrate knowledge. The Science Test contains 40 questions that require interpreting data, understanding scientific investigations, and evaluating models and results.

The Writing Test is always given at the end of the exam so that test takers opting not to take it may leave after completing the other four subtests. This section consists of one essay in which students must analyze three different perspectives on a broad social issue and reconcile them in a cohesive essay. The following chart provides the breakdown of the sections of the ACT:

Subtest	Length	Number of Questions
English	45 minutes	75
Mathematics	60 minutes	60
Reading	35 minutes	40
Science	35 minutes	40
Writing (optional)	40 minutes	1 essay

Scoring

Score reports are typically available two weeks after the date of administration. Because there is no penalty for incorrect answers, test takers are encouraged to answer every question, even if they have to guess. For each of the four required subtests, test takers receive a score between 1 and 36. These scores are then averaged together to yield a Composite Score, which is the primary score reported as an "ACT score." The most prestigious colleges and universities are typically looking for Composite Scores greater than 30 in order to consider an applicant for admissions. Other selective schools typically expect candidates to have scores just under 30. Average institutions are more likely to set the bar lower (perhaps in the low 20s), while community colleges usually accept students with scores in the high teens. In 2016 and 2017, the mean Composite Score among all test takers (including those not applying to college) was 20.9.

The Writing Test is scored on a scale that ranges from 2 to 12 scale. In 2016 and 2017, the mean score was 6.7.

ACT English Test

Production of Writing

Topic Development

Rhetorical Aspects of Texts

An essay presents an idea to the reader from its author's perspective. The central assertion is stated in the first sentence of the essay, the thesis sentence. It is followed by paragraphs containing supporting ideas, which are developed by means of facts, details, and examples. The essay ends with a conclusion that paraphrases the thesis sentence, sums up the major points, and gives the reader a feeling of closure.

Identifying the Purpose of Different Parts of a Text

An essay contains a beginning, a middle, and an end. The purpose of the beginning, or introduction, is for the author to state the idea that she wants to explain in the middle, or body, of the essay. The body is where the author builds her argument with facts and examples that explain, support, and show the application of the thesis statement in the introduction, and by analyzing and interpreting the facts for the reader. In the end, or conclusion, the author restates the thesis and then brings the essay to a close by establishing the significance of the thesis in a larger context, or by posing a question that will compel further thought on the part of the reader.

Determining Whether a Text or Part of a Text has Met its Goal

An essay, or part of an essay, meets its goal by communicating an idea clearly and effectively to the reader. Clear communication is achieved through logical organization of the information that supports each main point. Arguments that are well thought out and communicated in a suitable tone are the foundations of effective communication. An essay has unity if all the parts relate to the thesis sentence, and it has coherence if the reader can follow the author's thoughts as they progress. If the reader is motivated, the essay has succeeded.

Evaluating the Relevance of Material in Terms of a Text's Focus

An essay should have its own internal logic, and each idea and element in it should fit together. If something doesn't fit, chances are it is irrelevant information that will distract the reader.

Organization, Unity, and Cohesion

Developing a Well-Organized Paragraph

A **paragraph** is a series of connected and related sentences addressing one topic. Writing good paragraphs benefits writers by helping them to stay on target while drafting and revising their work. It benefits readers by helping them to follow the writing more easily. Regardless of how brilliant their ideas may be, writers who do not present these ideas in organized ways will fail to engage readers—and fail to accomplish their writing goals. A fundamental rule for paragraphing is to confine each paragraph to a single idea. When writers find themselves transitioning to a new idea, they should start a new paragraph. However, a paragraph can include several pieces of evidence supporting its single idea, and it can include several points if they are all related to the overall paragraph topic. When writers find each point becoming lengthy, they may choose instead to devote a separate paragraph to every point and elaborate upon each more fully.

An effective paragraph should have the following elements:

- **Unity:** One major discussion point or focus should occupy the whole paragraph from beginning to end.

- **Coherence:** For readers to understand a paragraph, it must be coherent. Two components of coherence are logical and verbal bridges. In logical bridges, the writer may write consecutive sentences with parallel structure or carry an idea over across sentences. In verbal bridges, writers may repeat key words across sentences.

- A **topic sentence:** The paragraph should have a sentence that generally identifies the paragraph's thesis or main idea.

- Sufficient **development:** To develop a paragraph, writers can use the following techniques after stating their topic sentence:

    - Define terms

    - Cite data

    - Use illustrations, anecdotes, and examples

    - Evaluate causes and effects

    - Analyze the topic

    - Explain the topic using chronological order

A topic sentence identifies the main idea of the paragraph. Some are explicit, while some are implicit. The topic sentence can appear anywhere in the paragraph. However, many experts advise beginning writers to place each paragraph topic sentence at or near the beginning of its paragraph to ensure that their readers understand what the topic of each paragraph is. Even without having written an explicit topic sentence, the writer should still be able to summarize readily what subject matter each paragraph addresses. The writer must then fully develop the topic that is introduced or identified in the topic sentence. Depending on what the writer's purpose is, they may use different methods for developing each paragraph.

Two main steps in the process of organizing paragraphs and essays should both be completed after determining the writing's main point, while the writer is planning or outlining the work. The initial step is to give an order to the topics addressed in each paragraph. Writers must have logical reasons for putting one paragraph first, another second, etc. The second step is to sequence the sentences in each paragraph. As with the first step, writers must have logical reasons for the order of sentences. Sometimes the work's main point obviously indicates a specific order.

Topic Sentences

To be effective, a topic sentence should be concise so that readers get its point without losing the meaning among too many words. As an example, in *Only Yesterday: An Informal History of the 1920s* (1931), author Frederick Lewis Allen's topic sentence introduces his paragraph describing the 1929 stock market crash: "The Bull Market was dead." This example illustrates the criteria of conciseness and brevity. It is also a strong sentence, expressed clearly and unambiguously. The topic sentence also introduces the paragraph, alerting the reader's attention to the main idea of the paragraph and the subject matter that follows the topic sentence.

Experts often recommend opening a paragraph with the topic sentence to enable the reader to realize the main point of the paragraph immediately. Application letters for jobs and university admissions also benefit from opening with topic sentences. However, positioning the topic sentence at the end of a paragraph is more logical when the paragraph identifies a number of specific details that accumulate evidence and then culminates with a generalization. While paragraphs with extremely obvious main ideas need no topic sentences, more often—and particularly for students learning to write—the topic sentence is the most important sentence in the paragraph. It not only communicates the main idea quickly to readers, but it also helps writers produce and control information.

Knowledge of Language

Context Clues

Readers can often figure out what unfamiliar words mean without interrupting their reading to look them up in dictionaries by examining context. **Context** includes the other words or sentences in a passage. One common context clue is the root word and any affixes (prefixes/suffixes). Another common context clue is a synonym or definition included in the sentence. Sometimes both exist in the same sentence. Here's an example:

> Scientists who study birds are *ornithologists*.

Many readers may not know the word *ornithologist*. However, the example contains a definition (scientists who study birds). The reader may also have the ability to analyze the suffix (*-logy*, meaning the study of) and root (*ornitho-*, meaning bird).

Another common context clue is a sentence that shows differences. Here's an example:

> Birds *incubate* their eggs outside of their bodies, unlike mammals.

Some readers may be unfamiliar with the word *incubate*. However, since we know that "unlike mammals," birds incubate their eggs outside of their bodies, we can infer that *incubate* has something to do with keeping eggs warm outside the body until they are hatched.

In addition to analyzing the etymology of a word's root and affixes and extrapolating word meaning from sentences that contrast an unknown word with an antonym, readers can also determine word meanings from sentence context clues based on logic. Here's an example:

> Birds are always looking out for predators that could attack their young.

The reader who is unfamiliar with the word *predator* could determine from the context of the sentence that predators usually prey upon baby birds and possibly other young animals. Readers might also use the context clue of etymology here, as *predator* and *prey* have the same root.

Analyzing Word Parts

By learning some of the etymologies of words and their parts, readers can break new words down into components and analyze their combined meanings. For example, the root word *soph* is Greek for wise or knowledge. Knowing this informs the meanings of English words including *sophomore, sophisticated,* and *philosophy*. Those who also know that *phil* is Greek for love will realize that *philosophy* means the love of knowledge. They can then extend this knowledge of *phil* to understand *philanthropist* (one who loves people), *bibliophile* (book lover), *philharmonic* (loving harmony), *hydrophilic* (water-loving), and so on. In addition, *phob-* derives from the Greek *phobos,* meaning fear. This informs all words ending with it as meaning fear of various things: *acrophobia* (fear of heights), *arachnophobia* (fear of spiders), *claustrophobia* (fear of enclosed spaces), *ergophobia* (fear of work), and *hydrophobia* (fear of water), among others.

Some English word origins from other languages, like ancient Greek, are found in large numbers and varieties of English words. An advantage of the shared ancestry of these words is that once readers recognize the meanings of some Greek words or word roots, they can determine or at least get an idea of what many different English words mean. As an example, the Greek word *métron* means to measure, a measure, or something used to measure; the English word meter derives from it. Knowing this informs many other English words, including *altimeter, barometer, diameter, hexameter, isometric,* and *metric.* While readers must know the meanings of the other parts of these words to decipher their meaning fully, they already have an idea that they are all related in some way to measures or measuring.

While all English words ultimately derive from a proto-language known as Indo-European, many of them historically came into the developing English vocabulary later, from sources like the ancient Greeks' language, the Latin used throughout Europe and much of the Middle East during the reign of the Roman Empire, and the Anglo-Saxon languages used by England's early tribes. In addition to classic revivals and native foundations, by the Renaissance era other influences included French, German, Italian, and Spanish. Today we can often discern English word meanings by knowing common roots and affixes, particularly from Greek and Latin.

The following is a list of common prefixes and their meanings:

Prefix	Definition	Examples
a-	without	atheist, agnostic
ad-	to, toward	advance
ante-	before	antecedent, antedate
anti-	opposing	antipathy, antidote
auto-	self	autonomy, autobiography
bene-	well, good	benefit, benefactor
bi-	two	bisect, biennial
bio-	life	biology, biosphere
chron-	time	chronometer, synchronize
circum-	around	circumspect, circumference
com-	with, together	commotion, complicate
contra-	against, opposing	contradict, contravene
cred-	belief, trust	credible, credit
de-	from	depart
dem-	people	demographics, democracy
dis-	away, off, down, not	dissent, disappear
equi-	equal, equally	equivalent
ex-	former, out of	extract
for-	away, off, from	forget, forswear
fore-	before, previous	foretell, forefathers
homo-	same, equal	homogenized
hyper-	excessive, over	hypercritical, hypertension

Prefix	Definition	Examples
in-	in, into	intrude, invade
inter-	among, between	intercede, interrupt
mal-	bad, poorly, not	malfunction
micr-	small	microbe, microscope
mis-	bad, poorly, not	misspell, misfire
mono-	one, single	monogamy, monologue
mor-	die, death	mortality, mortuary
neo-	new	neolithic, neoconservative
non-	not	nonentity, nonsense
omni-	all, everywhere	omniscient
over-	above	overbearing
pan-	all, entire	panorama, pandemonium
para-	beside, beyond	parallel, paradox
phil-	love, affection	philosophy, philanthropic
poly-	many	polymorphous, polygamous
pre-	before, previous	prevent, preclude
prim-	first, early	primitive, primary
pro-	forward, in place of	propel, pronoun
re-	back, backward, again	revoke, recur
sub-	under, beneath	subjugate, substitute
super-	above, extra	supersede, supernumerary
trans-	across, beyond, over	transact, transport
ultra-	beyond, excessively	ultramodern, ultrasonic, ultraviolet
un-	not, reverse of	unhappy, unlock
vis-	to see	visage, visible

The following is a list of common suffixes and their meanings:

Suffix	Definition	Examples
-able	likely, able to	capable, tolerable
-ance	act, condition	acceptance, vigilance
-ard	one that does excessively	drunkard, wizard
-ation	action, state	occupation, starvation
-cy	state, condition	accuracy, captaincy
-er	one who does	teacher
-esce	become, grow, continue	convalesce, acquiesce
-esque	in the style of, like	picturesque, grotesque
-ess	feminine	waitress, lioness
-ful	full of, marked by	thankful, zestful
-ible	able, fit	edible, possible, divisible
-ion	action, result, state	union, fusion
-ish	suggesting, like	churlish, childish
-ism	act, manner, doctrine	barbarism, socialism
-ist	doer, believer	monopolist, socialist

Suffix	Definition	Examples
-ition	action, result, state,	sedition, expedition
-ity	quality, condition	acidity, civility
-ize	cause to be, treat with	sterilize, mechanize, criticize
-less	lacking, without	hopeless, countless
-like	like, similar	childlike, dreamlike
-ly	like, of the nature of	friendly, positively
-ment	means, result, action	refreshment, disappointment
-ness	quality, state	greatness, tallness
-or	doer, office, action	juror, elevator, honor
-ous	marked by, given to	religious, riotous
-some	apt to, showing	tiresome, lonesome
-th	act, state, quality	warmth, width
-ty	quality, state	enmity, activity

Conventions of Standard English Spelling

Homophones

Homophones are words that have different meanings and spellings, but sound the same. These can be confusing for English Language Learners (ELLs) and beginning students, but even native English-speaking adults can find them problematic unless informed by context. Whereas listeners must rely entirely on context to differentiate spoken homophone meanings, readers with good spelling knowledge have a distinct advantage since homophones are spelled differently. For instance, *their* means belonging to them; *there* indicates location; and *they're* is a contraction of *they are*; despite different meanings, they all sound the same. *Lacks* can be a plural noun or a present-tense, third-person singular verb; either way it refers to absence—*deficiencies* as a plural noun, and *is deficient in* as a verb. But *lax* is an adjective that means loose, slack, relaxed, uncontrolled, or negligent. These two spellings, derivations, and meanings are completely different. With speech, listeners cannot know spelling and must use context; however, with print, readers with spelling knowledge can differentiate them with or without context.

Homonyms, Homophones, and Homographs

Homophones are words that sound the same in speech, but have different spellings and meanings. For example, *to, too,* and *two* all sound alike, but have three different spellings and meanings. Homophones with different spellings are also called **heterographs. Homographs** are words that are spelled identically, but have different meanings. If they also have different pronunciations, they are **heteronyms**. For instance, *tear* pronounced one way means a drop of liquid formed by the eye; pronounced another way, it means to rip. Homophones that are also homographs are **homonyms**. For example, *bark* can mean the outside of a tree or a dog's vocalization; both meanings have the same spelling. *Stalk* can mean a plant stem or to pursue and/or harass somebody; these are spelled and pronounced the same. *Rose* can mean a flower or the past tense of *rise*. Many non-linguists confuse things by using "homonym" to mean sets of words that are homophones but not homographs, and also those that are homographs but not homophones.

The word *row* can mean to use oars to propel a boat; a linear arrangement of objects or print; or an argument. It is pronounced the same with the first two meanings, but differently with the third. Because it is spelled identically regardless, all three meanings are homographs. However, the two meanings pronounced the same are homophones, whereas the one with the different pronunciation is a heteronym. By contrast, the word *read* means to peruse language, whereas the word *reed* refers to a marsh plant.

Because these are pronounced the same way, they are homophones; because they are spelled differently, they are heterographs. Homonyms are both homophones and homographs—pronounced and spelled identically, but with different meanings. One distinction between homonyms is of those with separate, unrelated etymologies, called "true" homonyms, e.g. *skate* meaning a fish or *skate* meaning to glide over ice/water. Those with common origins are called polysemes or polysemous homonyms, e.g. the *mouth* of an animal/human or of a river.

Irregular Plurals

One type of irregular English plural involves words that are spelled the same whether they are singular or plural. These include *deer, fish, salmon, trout, sheep, moose, offspring, species, aircraft,* etc. The spelling rule for making these words plural is simple: they do not change. Another type of irregular English plurals does change from singular to plural form, but it does not take regular English *–s* or *–es* endings. Their irregular plural endings are largely derived from grammatical and spelling conventions in the other languages of their origins, like Latin, German, and vowel shifts and other linguistic mutations. Some examples of these words and their irregular plurals include *child* and *children; die* and *dice; foot* and *feet; goose* and *geese; louse* and *lice; man* and *men; mouse* and *mice; ox* and *oxen; person* and *people; tooth* and *teeth;* and *woman* and *women.*

Contractions

Contractions are formed by joining two words together, omitting one or more letters from one of the component words, and replacing the omitted words with an apostrophe. An obvious yet often forgotten rule for spelling contractions is to place the apostrophe where the letters were omitted; for example, spelling errors like *did'nt* for *didn't. Didn't* is a contraction of *did not.* Therefore, the apostrophe replaces the "o" that is omitted from the "not" component. Another common error is confusing contractions with possessives because both include apostrophes, e.g. spelling the possessive *its* as "it's," which is a contraction of "it is"; spelling the possessive *their* as "they're," a contraction of "they are"; spelling the possessive *whose* as "who's," a contraction of "who is"; or spelling the possessive *your* as "you're," a contraction of "you are."

Frequently Misspelled Words

One source of spelling errors is not knowing whether to drop the final letter *e* from a word when its form is changed by adding an ending to indicate the past tense or progressive participle of a verb, converting an adjective to an adverb, a noun to an adjective, etc. Some words retain the final *e* when another syllable is added; others lose it. For example, *true* becomes *truly; argue* becomes *arguing; come* becomes *coming; write* becomes *writing;* and *judge* becomes *judging.* In these examples, the final *e* is dropped before adding the ending. But *severe* becomes *severely; complete* becomes *completely; sincere* becomes *sincerely; argue* becomes *argued;* and *care* becomes *careful.* In these instances, the final *e* is retained before adding the ending. Note that some words, like *argue* in these examples, drops the final *e* when the *–ing* ending is added to indicate the participial form; but the regular past tense ending of *–ed* makes it *argued,* in effect replacing the final *e* so that *arguing* is spelled without an *e* but *argued* is spelled with one.

Some English words contain the vowel combination of *ei,* while some contain the reverse combination of *ie.* Many people confuse these. Some examples include these:

> *ceiling, conceive, leisure, receive, weird, their, either, foreign, sovereign, neither, neighbors, seize, forfeit, counterfeit, height, weight, protein,* and *freight*

Words with *ie* include *piece, believe, chief, field, friend, grief, relief, mischief, siege, niece, priest, fierce, pierce, achieve, retrieve, hygiene, science,* and *diesel.* A rule that also functions as a mnemonic device is "I before E except after C, or when sounded like A as in 'neighbor' or 'weigh'." However, it is obvious from the list above that many exceptions exist.

Many people often misspell certain words by confusing whether they have the vowel *a, e,* or *i,* frequently in the middle syllable of three-syllable words or beginning the last syllables that sound the same in different words. For example, in the following correctly spelled words, the vowel in boldface is the one people typically get wrong by substituting one or either of the others for it:

> cem**e**tery, quant**i**ties, ben**e**fit, priv**i**lege, unpleas**a**nt, sep**a**rate, independ**e**nt, excell**e**nt, cat**e**gories, indispens**a**ble, and irrelev**a**nt

The words with final syllables that sound the same when spoken but are spelled differently include *unpleasant, independent, excellent,* and *irrelevant.* Another source of misspelling is whether or not to double consonants when adding suffixes. For example, we double the last consonant before *–ed* and *–ing* endings in *controlled, beginning, forgetting, admitted, occurred, referred,* and *hopping;* but we do not double the last consonant before the suffix in *shining, poured, sweating, loving, hating, smiling,* and *hoping.*

One way in which people misspell certain words frequently is by failing to include letters that are silent. Some letters are articulated when pronounced correctly but elided in some people's speech, which then transfers to their writing. Another source of misspelling is the converse: people add extraneous letters. For example, some people omit the silent *u* in *guarantee,* overlook the first *r* in *surprise,* leave out the *z* in *realize,* fail to double the *m* in *recommend,* leave out the middle *i* from *aspirin,* and exclude the *p* from *temperature.* The converse error, adding extra letters, is common in words like *until* by adding a second *l* at the end; or by inserting a superfluous syllabic *a* or *e* in the middle of *athletic,* reproducing a common mispronunciation.

Consistency in Style and Tone

To improve coherence and flow in a piece of writing, it is important for a writer to remain consistent in the style and tone used. The piece of writing should feel unified, and as if its author has maintained the same "voice" throughout. One way to ensure consistency in style and tone is maintained is to read the completed writing in its entirety in one sitting, "listening" for any deviations in word choice or structure that noticeably change the tone or style of the writing.

Conventions of Standard English

Sentence Structure and Formation

Four types of improper sentences are sentence fragments, run-on sentences, subject-verb and/or pronoun-antecedent disagreement, and non-parallel structure.

Sentence Fragments
Sentence fragments are caused by absent subjects, absent verbs, or dangling/uncompleted dependent clauses. Every sentence must have a subject and a verb to be complete. An example of a **fragment** is "Raining all night long," because there is no subject present. "It was raining all night long" is one correction. Another example of a sentence fragment is the second part in "Many scientists think in unusual ways. Einstein, for instance." The second phrase is a fragment because it has no verb. One correction is "Many scientists, like Einstein, think in unusual ways." Finally, look for "cliffhanger" words like *if, when, because,* or *although* that introduce **dependent clauses**, which cannot stand alone without an

independent clause. For example, to correct the sentence fragment "If you get home early," add an independent clause: "If you get home early, we can go dancing."

Run-On Sentences

A run-on sentence combines two or more complete sentences without punctuating them correctly or separating them. For example, a run-on sentence caused by a lack of punctuation is the following:

> There is a malfunction in the computer system however there is nobody available right now who knows how to troubleshoot it.

One correction is, "There is a malfunction in the computer system; however, there is nobody available right now who knows how to troubleshoot it." Another is, "There is a malfunction in the computer system. However, there is nobody available right now who knows how to troubleshoot it."

An example of a **comma splice** of two sentences is the following:

> Jim decided not to take the bus, he walked home.

Replacing the comma with a period or a semicolon corrects this. Commas that try and separate two independent clauses without a contraction are considered comma splices.

Parallel Sentence Structures

Parallel structure in a sentence matches the forms of sentence components. Any sentence containing more than one description or phrase should keep them consistent in wording and form. Readers can easily follow writers' ideas when they are written in parallel structure, making it an important element of correct sentence construction. For example, this sentence lacks parallelism: "Our coach is a skilled manager, a clever strategist, and works hard." The first two phrases are parallel, but the third is not. Correction: "Our coach is a skilled manager, a clever strategist, and a hard worker." Now all three phrases match in form. Here is another example:

> Fred intercepted the ball, escaped tacklers, and a touchdown was scored.

This is also non-parallel. Here is the sentence corrected:

> Fred intercepted the ball, escaped tacklers, and scored a touchdown.

Sentence Fluency

For fluent composition, writers must use a variety of sentence types and structures, and also ensure that they smoothly flow together when they are read. To accomplish this, they must first be able to identify fluent writing when they read it. This includes being able to distinguish among simple, compound, complex, and compound-complex sentences in text; to observe variations among sentence types, lengths, and beginnings; and to notice figurative language and understand how it augments sentence length and imparts musicality. Once writers recognize superior fluency, they should revise their own writing to be more readable and fluent. They must be able to apply acquired skills to revisions before being able to apply them to new drafts.

One strategy for revising writing to increase its sentence fluency is flipping sentences. This involves rearranging the word order in a sentence without deleting, changing, or adding any words. For example, the student or other writer who has written the sentence, "We went bicycling on Saturday" can revise it to, "On Saturday, we went bicycling." Another technique is using appositives. An **appositive** is a phrase or word that renames or identifies another adjacent word or phrase. Writers can revise for sentence fluency by inserting main phrases/words from one shorter sentence into another shorter sentence, combining them into one longer sentence, e.g. from "My cat Peanut is a gray and brown tabby. He loves hunting rats." to "My cat Peanut, a gray and brown tabby, loves hunting rats." Revisions can also connect shorter sentences by using conjunctions and commas and removing repeated words: "Scott likes eggs. Scott is allergic to eggs" becomes "Scott likes eggs, but he is allergic to them."

One technique for revising writing to increase sentence fluency is "padding" short, simple sentences by adding phrases that provide more details specifying why, how, when, and/or where something took place. For example, a writer might have these two simple sentences: "I went to the market. I purchased a cake." To revise these, the writer can add the following informative dependent and independent clauses and prepositional phrases, respectively: "Before my mother woke up, I sneaked out of the house and went to the supermarket. As a birthday surprise, I purchased a cake for her." When revising sentences to make them longer, writers must also punctuate them correctly to change them from simple sentences to compound, complex, or compound-complex sentences.

Skills Writers Can Employ to Increase Fluency
One way writers can increase fluency is by varying the beginnings of sentences. Writers do this by starting most of their sentences with different words and phrases rather than monotonously repeating the same ones across multiple sentences. Another way writers can increase fluency is by varying the lengths of sentences. Since run-on sentences are incorrect, writers make sentences longer by also converting them from simple to compound, complex, and compound-complex sentences. The coordination and subordination involved in these also give the text more variation and interest, hence more fluency. Here are a few more ways writers can increase fluency:

- Varying the transitional language and conjunctions used makes sentences more fluent.
- Writing sentences with a variety of rhythms by using prepositional phrases.
- Varying sentence structure adds fluency.

Punctuation

Rules of Capitalization
The first word of any document, and of each new sentence, is capitalized. Proper nouns, like names and adjectives derived from proper nouns, should also be capitalized. Here are some examples:

- Grand Canyon
- Pacific Palisades
- Golden Gate Bridge
- Freudian slip
- Shakespearian, Spenserian, or Petrarchan sonnet
- Irish song

Some exceptions are adjectives, originally derived from proper nouns, which through time and usage are no longer capitalized, like *quixotic, herculean,* or *draconian.* Capitals draw attention to specific instances of people, places, and things. Some categories that should be capitalized include the following:

- brand names
- companies
- weekdays
- months
- governmental divisions or agencies

- historical eras
- major historical events
- holidays
- institutions
- famous buildings
- ships and other manmade constructions
- natural and manmade landmarks
- territories
- nicknames
- epithets
- organizations
- planets
- nationalities
- tribes
- religions
- names of religious deities
- roads
- special occasions, like the Cannes Film Festival or the Olympic Games

Exceptions

Related to American government, capitalize the noun Congress but not the related adjective congressional. Capitalize the noun U.S. Constitution, but not the related adjective constitutional. Many experts advise leaving the adjectives federal and state in lowercase, as in *federal regulations* or *state water board*, and only capitalizing these when they are parts of official titles or names, like *Federal Communications Commission* or *State Water Resources Control Board*. While the names of the other planets in the solar system are capitalized as names, Earth is more often capitalized only when being described specifically as a planet, like *Earth's orbit*, but lowercase otherwise since it is used not only as a proper noun but also to mean *land, ground, soil*, etc.

Names of animal species or breeds are not capitalized unless they include a proper noun. Then, only the proper noun is capitalized. *Antelope, black bear*, and *yellow-bellied sapsucker* are not capitalized. However, *Bengal tiger, German shepherd, Australian shepherd, French poodle*, and *Russian blue cat* are capitalized.

Other than planets, celestial bodies like the *sun, moon*, and *stars* are not capitalized. Medical conditions like *tuberculosis* or *diabetes* are lowercase; again, exceptions are proper nouns, like *Epstein-Barr syndrome, Alzheimer's disease*, and *Down syndrome*. Seasons and related terms like *winter solstice* or *autumnal equinox* are lowercase. Plants, including fruits and vegetables, like *poinsettia, celery*, or *avocado*, are not capitalized unless they include proper names, like *Douglas fir, Jerusalem artichoke, Damson plums*, or *Golden Delicious apples*.

Titles and Names

When official titles precede names, they should be capitalized, except when there is a comma between the title and name. But if a title follows or replaces a name, it should not be capitalized. For example, "the president" without a name is not capitalized, as in "The president addressed Congress." But with a name it is capitalized, like "President Obama addressed Congress." Or, "Chair of the Board Janet Yellen was appointed by President Obama." One exception is that some publishers and writers nevertheless capitalize President, Queen, Pope, etc., when these are not accompanied by names to show respect for these high offices. However, many writers in America object to this practice for violating democratic principles of equality. Occupations before full names are not capitalized, like owner Mark Cuban, director Martin Scorsese, or coach Roger McDowell.

Some universal rules for capitalization in composition titles include capitalizing the following:

- The first and last words of the title
- Forms of the verb *to be* and all other verbs
- Pronouns
- The word *not*

Universal rules for NOT capitalizing include the articles *the, a,* or *an;* the conjunctions *and, or,* or *nor,* and the preposition *to,* or *to* as part of the infinitive form of a verb. The exception to all of these is UNLESS any of them is the first or last word in the title, in which case they are capitalized. Other words are subject to differences of opinion and differences among various stylebooks or methods. These include *as, but, if,* and *or,* which some capitalize and others do not. Some authorities say no preposition should ever be capitalized; some say prepositions five or more letters long should be capitalized. The *Associated Press Stylebook* advises capitalizing prepositions longer than three letters (like *about, across,* or *with*).

Ellipses

Ellipses (. . .) signal omitted text when quoting. Some writers also use them to show a thought trailing off, but this should not be overused outside of dialogue. An example of an ellipses would be if someone is quoting a phrase out of a professional source but wants to omit part of the phrase that isn't needed: "Dr. Skim's analysis of pollen inside the body is clearly a myth . . . that speaks to the environmental guilt of our society."

Commas

Commas separate words or phrases in a series of three or more. The **Oxford comma** is the last comma in a series. Many people omit this last comma, but doing so often causes confusion. Here is an example:

> I love my sisters, the Queen of England and Madonna.

This example without the comma implies that the "Queen of England and Madonna" are the speaker's sisters. However, if the speaker was trying to say that they love their sisters, the Queen of England, as well as Madonna, there should be a comma after "Queen of England" to signify this.

Commas also separate two coordinate adjectives ("big, heavy dog") but not cumulative ones, which should be arranged in a particular order for them to make sense ("beautiful ancient ruins").

A comma ends the first of two independent clauses connected by conjunctions. Here is an example:

> I ate a bowl of tomato soup, and I was hungry very shortly after.

Here are some brief rules for commas:

- Commas follow introductory words like however, furthermore, well, why, and actually, among others.

- Commas go between a city and state: Houston, Texas.

- If using a comma between a surname and Jr. or Sr. or a degree like M.D., also follow the whole name with a comma: "Martin Luther King, Jr., wrote that."

- A comma follows a dependent clause beginning a sentence: "Although she was very small, . . ."

- Nonessential modifying words/phrases/clauses are enclosed by commas: "Wendy, who is Peter's sister, closed the window."

- Commas introduce or interrupt direct quotations: "She said, 'I hate him.' 'Why,' I asked, 'do you hate him?'"

Semicolons

Semicolons are used to connect two independent clauses, but should never be used in the place of a comma. They can replace periods between two closely connected sentences: "Call back tomorrow; it can wait until then." When writing items in a series and one or more of them contains internal commas, separate them with semicolons, like the following:

> People came from Springfield, Illinois; Alamo, Tennessee; Moscow, Idaho; and other locations.

Hyphens

Here are some rules concerning hyphens:

- Compound adjectives like *state-of-the-art* or *off-campus* are hyphenated.

- Original compound verbs and nouns are often hyphenated, like "throne-sat," "video-gamed," "no-meater."

- Adjectives ending in *–ly* are often hyphenated, like "family-owned" or "friendly-looking."

- "Five years old" is not hyphenated, but singular ages like "five-year-old" are.

- Hyphens can clarify. For example, in "stolen vehicle report," "stolen-vehicle report" clarifies that "stolen" modifies "vehicle," not "report."

- Compound numbers twenty-one through ninety-nine are spelled with hyphens.

- Prefixes before proper nouns/adjectives are hyphenated, like "mid-September" and "trans-Pacific."

Parentheses

Parentheses enclose information such as an aside or more clarifying information: "She ultimately replied (after deliberating for an hour) that she was undecided." They are also used to insert short, in-text definitions or acronyms: "His FBS (fasting blood sugar) was higher than normal." When parenthetical information ends the sentence, the period follows the parentheses: "We received new funds ($25,000)." Only put periods within parentheses if the whole sentence is inside them: "Look at this. (You'll be astonished.)" However, this can also be acceptable as a clause: "Look at this (you'll be astonished)." Although parentheses appear to be part of the sentence subject, they are not, and do not change subject-verb agreement: "Will (and his dog) was there."

Quotation Marks

Quotation marks are typically used when someone is quoting a direct word or phrase someone else writes or says. Additionally, quotation marks should be used for the titles of poems, short stories, songs, articles, chapters, and other shorter works. When quotations include punctuation, periods and commas should *always* be placed inside of the quotation marks.

When a quotation contains another quotation inside of it, the outer quotation should be enclosed in double quotation marks and the inner quotation should be enclosed in single quotation marks. For example: "Timmy was begging, 'Don't go! Don't leave!'" When using both double and single quotation marks, writers will find that many word-processing programs may automatically insert enough space between the single and double quotation marks to be visible for clearer reading. But if this is not the case, the writer should write/type them with enough space between to keep them from looking like three single quotation marks. Additionally, non-standard usages, terms used in an unusual fashion, and technical terms are often clarified by quotation marks. Here are some examples:

My "friend," Dr. Sims, has been micromanaging me again.

This way of extracting oil has been dubbed "fracking."

Apostrophes

One use of the apostrophe is followed by an *s* to indicate possession, like *Mrs. White's home* or *our neighbor's dog*. When using the *'s* after names or nouns that also end in the letter *s*, no single rule applies: some experts advise adding both the apostrophe and the *s*, like "the Jones's house," while others prefer using only the apostrophe and omitting the additional *s*, like "the Jones' house." The wisest expert advice is to pick one formula or the other and then apply it consistently. Newspapers and magazines often use *'s* after common nouns ending with *s*, but add only the apostrophe after proper nouns or names ending with *s*. One common error is to place the apostrophe before a name's final *s* instead of after it: "Ms. Hasting's book" is incorrect if the name is Ms. Hastings.

Plural nouns should not include apostrophes (e.g. "apostrophe's"). Exceptions are to clarify atypical plurals, like verbs used as nouns: "These are the do's and don'ts." Irregular plurals that do not end in *s* always take apostrophe-*s*, not *s*-apostrophe—a common error, as in "childrens' toys," which should be "children's toys." Compound nouns like mother-in-law, when they are singular and possessive, are followed by apostrophe-*s*, like "your mother-in-law's coat." When a compound noun is plural and possessive, the plural is formed before the apostrophe-*s*, like "your sisters-in-laws' coats." When two people named possess the same thing, use apostrophe-*s* after the second name only, like "Dennis and Pam's house."

Usage

Possessives

Possessive forms indicate possession, i.e. that something belongs to or is owned by someone or something. As such, the most common parts of speech to be used in possessive form are adjectives, nouns, and pronouns. The rule for correctly spelling/punctuating possessive nouns and proper nouns is with -*'s*, like "the woman's briefcase" or "Frank's hat." With possessive adjectives, however, apostrophes are not used: these include *my, your, his, her, its, our,* and *their*, like "my book," "your friend," "his car," "her house," "its contents," "our family," or "their property." Possessive pronouns include *mine, yours, his, hers, its, ours,* and *theirs*. These also have no apostrophes. The difference is that possessive adjectives take direct objects, whereas possessive pronouns replace them. For example, instead of using two possessive adjectives in a row, as in "I forgot my book, so Blanca let me use her book," which reads monotonously, replacing the second one with a possessive pronoun reads better: "I forgot my book, so Blanca let me use hers."

Pronouns

There are three pronoun cases: subjective case, objective case, and possessive case. Pronouns as subjects are pronouns that replace the subject of the sentence, such as *I, you, he, she, it, we, they* and *who*. Pronouns as objects replace the object of the sentence, such as *me, you, him, her, it, us, them,* and *whom*. Pronouns that show possession are *mine, yours, hers, its, ours, theirs,* and *whose*. The following are examples of different pronoun cases:

- Subject pronoun: *She* ate the cake for her birthday. *I* saw the movie.
- Object pronoun: You gave *me* the card last weekend. She gave the picture to *him*.
- Possessive pronoun: That bracelet you found yesterday is *mine*. *His* name was Casey.

Adjectives

Adjectives are descriptive words that modify nouns or pronouns. They may occur before or after the nouns or pronouns they modify in sentences. For example, in "This is a big house," *big* is an adjective modifying or describing the noun *house*. In "This house is big," the adjective is at the end of the sentence rather than preceding the noun it modifies.

A rule of punctuation that applies to adjectives is to separate a series of adjectives with commas. For example, "Their home was a large, rambling, old, white, two-story house." A comma should never separate the last adjective from the noun, though.

Adverbs

Whereas adjectives modify and describe nouns or pronouns, adverbs modify and describe adjectives, verbs, or other adverbs. Adverbs can be thought of as answers to questions in that they describe when, where, how, how often, how much, or to what extent.

Many (but not all) adjectives can be converted to adverbs by adding *–ly*. For example, in "She is a quick learner," *quick* is an adjective modifying *learner*. In "She learns quickly," *quickly* is an adverb modifying *learns*. One exception is *fast*. *Fast* is an adjective in "She is a fast learner." However, *–ly* is never added to the word *fast*; it retains the same form as an adverb in "She learns fast."

Verbs

A verb is a word or phrase that expresses action, feeling, or state of being. Verbs explain what their subject is *doing*. Three different types of verbs used in a sentence are action verbs, linking verbs, and helping verbs.

Action verbs show a physical or mental action. Some examples of action verbs are *play, type, jump, write, examine, study, invent, develop,* and *taste*. The following example uses an action verb:

> Kat *imagines* that she is a mermaid in the ocean.

The verb *imagines* explains what Kat is doing: she is imagining being a mermaid.

Linking verbs connect the subject to the predicate without expressing an action. The following sentence shows an example of a linking verb:

> The mango *tastes* sweet.

The verb *tastes* is a linking verb. The mango doesn't *do* the tasting, but the word *taste* links the mango to its predicate, sweet. Most linking verbs can also be used as action verbs, such as *smell, taste, look, seem, grow,* and *sound*. Saying something *is* something else is also an example of a linking verb. For example, if we were to say, "Peaches is a dog," the verb *is* would be a linking verb in this sentence, since it links the subject to its predicate.

Helping verbs are verbs that help the main verb in a sentence. Examples of helping verbs are *be, am, is, was, have, has, do, did, can, could, may, might, should,* and *must,* among others. The following are examples of helping verbs:

> Jessica *is* planning a trip to Hawaii.

> Brenda *does* not like camping.

> Xavier *should* go to the dance tonight.

Notice that after each of these helping verbs is the main verb of the sentence: *planning, like,* and *go.* Helping verbs usually show an aspect of time.

Transitional Words and Phrases
In connected writing, some sentences naturally lead to others, whereas in other cases, a new sentence expresses a new idea. We use transitional phrases to connect sentences and the ideas they convey. This makes the writing coherent. Transitional language also guides the reader from one thought to the next. For example, when pointing out an objection to the previous idea, starting a sentence with "However," "But," or "On the other hand" is transitional. When adding another idea or detail, writers use "Also," "In addition," "Furthermore," "Further," "Moreover," "Not only," etc. Readers have difficulty perceiving connections between ideas without such transitional wording.

Subject-Verb Agreement
Lack of subject-verb agreement is a very common grammatical error. One of the most common instances is when people use a series of nouns as a compound subject with a singular instead of a plural verb. Here is an example:

> Identifying the best books, locating the sellers with the lowest prices, and paying for them *is* difficult

instead of saying "*are* difficult." Additionally, when a sentence subject is compound, the verb is plural:

> He and his cousins *were* at the reunion.

However, if the conjunction connecting two or more singular nouns or pronouns is "or" or "nor," the verb must be singular to agree:

> That pen or another one like it is in the desk drawer.

If a compound subject includes both a singular noun and a plural one, and they are connected by "or" or "nor," the verb must agree with the subject closest to the verb: "Sally or her sisters go jogging daily"; but "Her sisters or Sally goes jogging daily."

Simply put, singular subjects require singular verbs and plural subjects require plural verbs. A common source of agreement errors is not identifying the sentence subject correctly. For example, people often write sentences incorrectly like, "The group of students *were* complaining about the test." The subject is not the plural "students" but the singular "group." Therefore, the correct sentence should read, "The group of students *was* complaining about the test." The converse also applies, for example, in this incorrect sentence: "The facts in that complicated court case *is* open to question." The subject of the sentence is not the singular "case" but the plural "facts." Hence the sentence would correctly be written: "The facts in that complicated court case *are* open to question." New writers should not be misled by the distance between the subject and verb, especially when another noun with a different number intervenes as in these examples. The verb must agree with the subject, not the noun closest to it.

Pronoun-Antecedent Agreement

Pronouns within a sentence must refer specifically to one noun, known as the **antecedent.** Sometimes, if there are multiple nouns within a sentence, it may be difficult to ascertain which noun belongs to the pronoun. It's important that the pronouns always clearly reference the nouns in the sentence so as not to confuse the reader. Here's an example of an unclear pronoun reference:

After Catherine cut Libby's hair, David bought her some lunch.

The pronoun in the examples above is *her*. The pronoun could either be referring to *Catherine* or *Libby*. Here are some ways to write the above sentence with a clear pronoun reference:

After Catherine cut Libby's hair, David bought Libby some lunch.

David bought Libby some lunch after Catherine cut Libby's hair.

But many times the pronoun will clearly refer to its antecedent, like the following:

After David cut Catherine's hair, he bought her some lunch.

Formal and Informal Language

Formal language is less personal than informal language. It is more "buttoned-up" and business-like, adhering to proper grammatical rules. It is used in professional or academic contexts, to convey respect or authority. For example, one would use formal language to write an informative or argumentative essay for school or to address a superior. Formal language avoids contractions, slang, colloquialisms, and first-person pronouns. Formal language uses sentences that are usually more complex and often in passive voice. Punctuation can differ as well. For example, **exclamation points (!)** are used to show strong emotion or can be used as an interjection but should be used sparingly in formal writing situations.

Informal language is often used when communicating with family members, friends, peers, and those known more personally. It is more casual, spontaneous, and forgiving in its conformity to grammatical rules and conventions. Informal language is used for personal emails and correspondence between coworkers or other familial relationships. The tone is more relaxed. In informal writing, slang, contractions, clichés, and the first- and second-person are often used.

ACT Reading Test

Key Ideas and Details

Central Ideas and Themes

The **topic** of a text is the general subject matter. Text topics can usually be expressed in one word, or a few words at most. Additionally, readers should ask themselves what point the author is trying to make. This point is the **main idea** of the text, the one thing the author wants readers to know concerning the topic. Once the author has established the main idea, he or she will support the main idea by supporting details. **Supporting details** are evidence that support the main idea and include personal testimonies, examples, or statistics.

One analogy for these components and their relationships is that a text is like a well-designed house. The topic is the roof, covering all rooms. The main idea is the frame. The supporting details are the various rooms. To identify the topic of a text, readers can ask themselves what or who the author is writing about in the paragraph. To locate the main idea, readers can ask themselves what one idea the author wants readers to know about the topic. To identify supporting details, readers can put the main idea into question form and ask, "what does the author use to prove or explain their main idea?"

Let's look at an example. An author is writing an essay about the Amazon rainforest and trying to convince the audience that more funding should go into protecting the area from deforestation. The author makes the argument stronger by including evidence of the benefits of the rainforest: it provides habitats to a variety of species, it provides much of the earth's oxygen which in turn cleans the atmosphere, and it is the home to medicinal plants that may be the answer to some of the world's deadliest diseases. Here is an outline of the essay looking at topic, main idea, and supporting details:

- Topic: Amazon rainforest
- Main Idea: The Amazon rainforest should receive more funding to protect it from deforestation.
- Supporting Details:
    - 1. It provides habitats to a variety of species
    - 2. It provides much of the earth's oxygen which in turn cleans the atmosphere
    - 3. It is home to medicinal plants that may be the answer to some of the deadliest diseases.

Notice that the topic of the essay is listed in a few key words: "Amazon rainforest." The main idea tells us what about the topic is important: that the topic should be funded in order to prevent deforestation. Finally, the supporting details are what author relies on to convince the audience to act or to believe in the truth of the main idea.

Summarizing Information and Ideas

An important skill is the ability to read a complex text and then reduce its length and complexity by focusing on the key events and details. A **summary** is a shortened version of the original text, written by the reader in their own words. The summary should be shorter than the original text, and it must be thoughtfully formed to include critical points from the original text.

In order to effectively summarize a complex text, it's necessary to understand the original source and identify the major points covered. It may be helpful to outline the original text to get the big picture and avoid getting bogged down in the minor details. For example, a summary wouldn't include a statistic from the original source unless it was the major focus of the text. It's also important for readers to use their own words, yet retain the original meaning of the passage. The key to a good summary is emphasizing the main idea without changing the focus of the original information.

The more complex a text, the more difficult it can be to summarize. Readers must evaluate all points from the original source and then filter out what they feel are the less necessary details. Only the essential ideas should remain. The summary often mirrors the original text's organizational structure. For example, in a problem-solution text structure, the author typically presents readers with a problem and then develops solutions through the course of the text. An effective summary would likely retain this general structure, rephrasing the problem and then reporting the most useful or plausible solutions.

Paraphrasing is somewhat similar to summarizing. It calls for the reader to take a small part of the passage and list or describe its main points. Paraphrasing is more than rewording the original passage, though. Like summary, it should be written in the reader's own words, while still retaining the meaning of the original source. The main difference between summarizing and paraphrasing is that a summary would be appropriate for a much larger text, while paraphrase might focus on just a few lines of text. Effective paraphrasing will indicate an understanding of the original source, yet still help the reader expand on their interpretation. A paraphrase should neither add new information nor remove essential facts that change the meaning of the source.

Understanding Relationships

In order to better comprehend more complex texts, readers strive to draw connections between ideas or events. Authors often have a main idea or argument that is supported by ideas, facts, or expert opinion. These relationships that are built into writing can take on several different forms.

Depending on the main argument of an informational text, authors may choose to employ a variety of relationship techniques. But before relationships can be developed in writing, the author needs to get organized. What is the main idea or argument? How does the author plan to support that idea? Once the author has a clear picture of what they would like to focus on, they need to build transitions from one idea to the next. Learning the importance of transitioning from one sentence to another, from one paragraph to another, and from one idea to another will not only strengthen the validity of the writing but will also enhance the reader's comprehension.

When transitioning from one sentence to another, authors employ specific connecting words that emphasize the relationships between sentences. Taking the time to consider these transitional words can make the difference between a choppy or confusing paragraph and a well-written one. Consider the following:

> When I was growing up, the neighborhood had kids at every turn. I lived in a townhouse then. In my adult years, I live in a quiet suburb with hardly any children.

> When I was growing up, I lived in a neighborhood where there were kids at every turn. In contrast to my younger years, my adult years are unfolding in a quiet suburb with hardly any children.

Notice how the first example, although written coherently, employs sentences that are somehow disjointed. The transition between the statements is far from smooth. However, in the second example, the simple addition of the phrase "in contrast" connects the two parts of the writer's life and allows the reader to fully comprehend the text.

Learning to transition from sentence to sentence, from paragraph to paragraph, and throughout any piece of writing is an essential skill that helps authors to demonstrate similarities, differences, and relationships, and it helps readers to strengthen comprehension.

Drawing Logical Inferences and Conclusions

Making an **inference** from a selection means to make an educated guess from the passage read. Inferences should be conclusions based off of sound evidence and reasoning. When multiple-choice test questions ask about the logical conclusion that can be drawn from reading text, the test taker must identify which choice will unavoidably lead to that conclusion. In order to eliminate the incorrect choices, the test taker should come up with a hypothetical situation wherein an answer choice is true, but the conclusion is not true. For example, here is an example with three answer choices:

> Fred purchased the newest PC available on the market. Therefore, he purchased the most expensive PC in the computer store.
>
> What can one assume for this conclusion to follow logically?
>
> a. Fred enjoys purchasing expensive items.
> b. PCs are some of the most expensive personal technology products available.
> c. The newest PC is the most expensive one.

The premise of the text is the first sentence: Fred purchased the newest PC. The conclusion is the second sentence: Fred purchased the most expensive PC. Recent release and price are two different factors; the difference between them is the logical gap. To eliminate the gap, one must equate whatever new information the conclusion introduces with the pertinent information the premise has stated. This example simplifies the process by having only one of each: one must equate product recency with product price. Therefore, a possible bridge to the logical gap could be a sentence stating that the newest PCs always cost the most.

Making Predictions and Inferences
One technique authors often use to make their fictional stories more interesting is not giving away too much information by providing hints and description. It is then up to the reader to draw a conclusion about the author's meaning by connecting textual clues with the reader's own pre-existing experiences and knowledge. Drawing conclusions is an important reading strategy for understanding what is occurring in a text. Rather than directly stating who, what, where, when, or why, authors often describe story elements. Then, readers must draw conclusions to understand significant story components. As they go through a text, readers can think about the setting, characters, plot, problem, and solution; whether the author provided any clues for consideration; and combine any story clues with their existing knowledge and experiences to draw conclusions about what occurs in the text.

Making Predictions
Before and during reading, readers can apply the reading strategy of making predictions about what they think may happen next. For example, what plot and character developments will occur in fiction? What points will the author discuss in nonfiction? Making predictions about portions of text they have not yet

read prepares readers mentally for reading, and also gives them a purpose for reading. To inform and make predictions about text, the reader can do the following:

- Consider the title of the text and what it implies
- Look at the cover of the book
- Look at any illustrations or diagrams for additional visual information
- Analyze the structure of the text
- Apply outside experience and knowledge to the text

Readers may adjust their predictions as they read. Reader predictions may or may not come true in text.

Making Inferences

Authors describe settings, characters, character emotions, and events. Readers must infer to understand text fully. Inferring enables readers to figure out meanings of unfamiliar words, make predictions about upcoming text, draw conclusions, and reflect on reading. Readers can infer about text before, during, and after reading. In everyday life, we use sensory information to infer. Readers can do the same with text. When authors do not answer all reader questions, readers must infer by saying "I think....This could be....This is because....Maybe....This means....I guess..." etc. Looking at illustrations, considering characters' behaviors, and asking questions during reading facilitate inference. Taking clues from text and connecting text to prior knowledge help to draw conclusions. Readers can infer word meanings, settings, reasons for occurrences, character emotions, pronoun referents, author messages, and answers to questions unstated in text. To practice inference, students can read sentences written/selected by the instructor, discuss the setting and character, draw conclusions, and make predictions.

Making inferences and drawing conclusions involve skills that are quite similar: both require readers to fill in information the author has omitted. Authors may omit information as a technique for inducing readers to discover the outcomes themselves; or they may consider certain information unimportant; or they may assume their reading audience already knows certain information. To make an inference or draw a conclusion about text, readers should observe all facts and arguments the author has presented and consider what they already know from their own personal experiences. Reading students taking multiple-choice tests that refer to text passages can determine correct and incorrect choices based on the information in the passage. For example, from a text passage describing an individual's signs of anxiety while unloading groceries and nervously clutching their wallet at a grocery store checkout, readers can infer or conclude that the individual may not have enough money to pay for everything.

Understanding Sequential, Comparative, and Cause-Effect Relationships

Recognizing Events in a Sequence

Sequence structure is the order of events in which a story or information is presented to the audience. Sometimes the text will be presented in chronological order, or sometimes it will be presented by displaying the most recent information first, then moving backwards in time. The sequence structure depends on the author, the context, and the audience. The structure of a text also depends on the genre in which the text is written. Is it literary fiction? Is it a magazine article? Is it instructions for how to complete a certain task? Different genres will have different purposes for switching up the sequence of their writing.

Narrative Structure

The structure presented in literary fiction is also known as **narrative structure**. Narrative structure is the foundation on which the text moves. The basic ways for moving the text along are in the plot and the setting. The plot is the sequence of events in the narrative that move the text forward through cause and effect. The setting of a story is the place or time period in which the story takes place. Narrative structure has two main categories: linear and nonlinear.

Linear narrative is a narrative told in chronological order. Traditional linear narratives will follow the plot diagram below depicting the narrative arc. The narrative arc consists of the exposition, conflict, rising action, climax, falling action, and resolution.

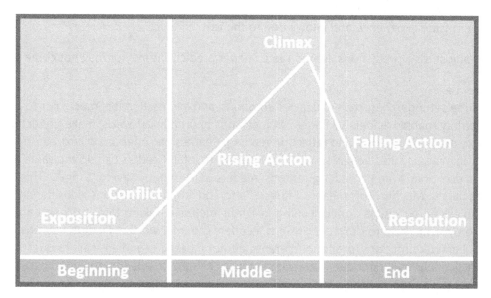

- Exposition: The exposition is in the beginning of a narrative and introduces the characters, setting, and background information of the story. The importance of the exposition lies in its framing of the upcoming narrative. Exposition literally means "a showing forth" in Latin.

- Conflict: The conflict, in a traditional narrative, is presented toward the beginning of the story after the audience becomes familiar with the characters and setting. The conflict is a single instance between characters, nature, or the self, in which the central character is forced to make a decision or move forward with some kind of action. The conflict presents something for the main character, or protagonist, to overcome.

- Rising Action: The rising action is the part of the story that leads into the climax. The rising action will feature the development of characters and plot, and creates the tension and suspense that eventually lead to the climax.

- Climax: The climax is the part of the story where the tension produced in the rising action comes to a culmination. The climax is the peak of the story. In a traditional structure, everything before the climax builds up to it, and everything after the climax falls from it. It is the height of the narrative, and is usually either the most exciting part of the story or is marked by some turning point in the character's journey.

- Falling Action: The falling action happens as a result of the climax. Characters continue to develop, although there is a wrapping up of loose ends here. The falling action leads to the resolution.

- Resolution: The resolution is where the story comes to an end and usually leaves the reader with the satisfaction of knowing what happened within the story and why. However, stories do not always end in this fashion. Sometimes readers can be confused or frustrated at the end from lack of information or the absence of a happy ending.

A **nonlinear narrative** deviates from the traditional narrative in that it does not always follow the traditional plot structure of the narrative arc. Nonlinear narratives may include structures that are disjointed, circular, or disruptive, in the sense that they do not follow chronological order, but rather a nontraditional order of structure. *In medias res* is an example of a structure that predates the linear narrative. *In medias res* is Latin for "in the middle of things," which is how many ancient texts, especially epic poems, began their story, such as Homer's *Iliad*. Instead of having a clear exposition with a full development of characters, they would begin right in the middle of the action.

Modernist texts in the late nineteenth and early twentieth century are known for their experimentation with disjointed narratives, moving away from traditional linear narrative. Disjointed narratives are depicted in novels like *Catch 22*, where the author, Joseph Heller, structures the narrative based on free association of ideas rather than chronology. Another nonlinear narrative can be seen in the novel *Wuthering Heights*, written by Emily Bronte, which disrupts the chronological order by being told retrospectively after the first chapter. There seem to be two narratives in *Wuthering Heights* working at the same time: a present narrative as well as a past narrative. Authors employ disrupting narratives for various reasons; some use it for the purpose of creating situational irony for the readers, while some use it to create a certain effect in the reader, such as excitement, or even a feeling of discomfort or fear.

Sequence Structure in Technical Documents

The purpose of technical documents, such as instructions manuals, cookbooks, or "user-friendly" documents, is to provide information to users as clearly and efficiently as possible. In order to do this, the sequence structure in technical documents that should be used is one that is as straightforward as possible. This usually involves some kind of chronological order or a direct sequence of events. For example, someone who is reading an instruction manual on how to set up their Smart TV wants directions in a clear, simple, straightforward manner that does not leave the reader to guess at the proper sequence or lead to confusion.

Sequence Structure in Informational Texts

The structure in informational texts depends again on the genre. For example, a newspaper article may start by stating an exciting event that happened, and then move on to talk about that event in chronological order. Many informational texts also use **cause and effect structure**, which describes an event and then identifies reasons for why that event occurred. Some essays may write about their subjects by way of **comparison and contrast**, which is a structure that compares two things or contrasts them to highlight their differences. Other documents, such as proposals, will have a **problem to solution structure**, where the document highlights some kind of problem and then offers a solution toward the end. Finally, some informational texts are written with lush details and description in order to captivate the audience, allowing them to visualize the information presented to them. This type of structure is known as **descriptive**.

Comparative and Cause-and-Effect Relationships

Authors employ the compare and contrast strategy to point out the differences or similarities between two subjects. Readers must learn to use comparative thinking to comprehend and evaluate these similarities and differences, but readers have been using comparative thinking throughout their lives. Humans naturally compare and contrast in their everyday lives. Do we relate better to our mothers or our fathers? Should we attend the local college or the out-of-state option? Is it better to own a cat or a dog?

Throughout our lives, people compare and contrast, and in writing, it is no different. Consider the following sentence:

> Although it has been common practice in the United States to encourage the consumption of meat in order to ensure adequate protein levels, more and more people are turning to a plant-based diet, which, they argue, contains healthy levels of protein.

Clearly, the author is comparing and contrasting the two ways in which humans can absorb protein—from meat or from plant-based foods. When students read material that is being compared and contrasted, they begin to use higher-level thinking. The compare and contrast strategy helps readers analyze pairs of ideas, opinions, arguments, or facts, and it improves comprehension by emphasizing important details. Comparing and contrasting can make abstract ideas more concrete, and comparing and contrasting can even strengthen a student's writing skills. Comparing and contrasting helps readers organize information and develop their ideas with greater clarity.

Another common writing strategy involves cause and effect. Cause and effect may be the most recognizable of these relationships and is often used in informational texts. The "cause" refers to the reason why something happened, and the "effect" refers to what happened as a result of the cause. Consider the following sentences:

> I was late for work.

> My alarm was not set.

There is clearly a relationship between these two sentences. The cause of the individual's having been late for work was the unset alarm. The effect the unset alarm had was the individual's arriving late for work. In order to connect these two sentences into a cause-and-effect sentence, an author could write:

> Since my alarm was not set, I was late for work.

Some of the most commonly used keywords that help to identify cause-and-effect relationships in writing include, *because, since, so, if, then, before*, and, *after*. But authors do not always make the relationship this simple to detect. Oftentimes, the cause follows the effect. Consider the following sentence:

> The college tuition significantly decreased after the government's announcement of improved funding.

The cause in this sentence is the government's announcement of improved funding. The effect of this improved funding is that college tuition has significantly decreased.

Understanding what happened and why helps to strengthen reading comprehension, develop skills that identify patterns in writing, and enhances the ability to explain and analyze the writing.

Craft and Structure

Determining Word and Phrase Meanings

When readers encounter an unfamiliar word in text, they can use the surrounding context—the overall subject matter, specific chapter/section topic, and especially the immediate sentence context. Among others, one category of context clues is grammar. For example, the position of a word in a sentence and its relationship to the other words can help the reader establish whether the unfamiliar word is a verb, a noun, an adjective, an adverb, etc. This narrows down the possible meanings of the word to one part of speech. However, this may be insufficient. In a sentence that many birds *migrate* twice yearly, the reader can determine the word is a verb, and probably does not mean eat or drink; but it could mean travel, mate, lay eggs, hatch, molt, etc.

Some words can have a number of different meanings depending on how they are used. For example, the word *fly* has a different meaning in each of the following sentences:

- "His trousers have a fly on them."
- "He swatted the fly on his trousers."
- "Those are some fly trousers."
- "They went fly fishing."
- "She hates to fly."
- "If humans were meant to fly, they would have wings."

As strategies, readers can try substituting a familiar word for an unfamiliar one and see whether it makes sense in the sentence. They can also identify other words in a sentence, offering clues to an unfamiliar word's meaning.

Readers can often figure out what unfamiliar words mean without interrupting their reading to look them up in dictionaries by examining context. **Context** includes the other words or sentences in a passage. One common context clue is the root word and any affixes (prefixes/suffixes). Another common context clue is a synonym or definition included in the sentence. Sometimes both exist in the same sentence. Here's an example:

Scientists who study birds are *ornithologists*.

Many readers may not know the word *ornithologist*. However, the example contains a definition (scientists who study birds). The reader may also have the ability to analyze the suffix (*-logy*, meaning the study of) and root (*ornitho-*, meaning bird).

Another common context clue is a sentence that shows differences. Here's an example:

Birds *incubate* their eggs outside of their bodies, unlike mammals.

Some readers may be unfamiliar with the word *incubate*. However, since we know that "unlike mammals," birds incubate their eggs outside of their bodies, we can infer that *incubate* has something to do with keeping eggs warm outside the body until they are hatched.

In addition to analyzing the etymology of a word's root and affixes and extrapolating word meaning from sentences that contrast an unknown word with an antonym, readers can also determine word meanings from sentence context clues based on logic.

Here's an example:

Birds are always looking out for predators that could attack their young.

The reader who is unfamiliar with the word *predator* could determine from the context of the sentence that predators usually prey upon baby birds and possibly other young animals. Readers might also use the context clue of etymology here, as *predator* and *prey* have the same root.

Denotation and Connotation

Denotation refers to a word's explicit definition, like that found in the dictionary. Denotation is often set in comparison to connotation. **Connotation** is the emotional, cultural, social, or personal implication associated with a word. Denotation is more of an objective definition, whereas connotation can be more subjective, although many connotative meanings of words are similar for certain cultures. The denotative meanings of words are usually based on facts, and the connotative meanings of words are usually based on emotion. Here are some examples of words and their denotative and connotative meanings in Western culture:

Word	Denotative Meaning	Connotative Meaning
Home	A permanent place where one lives, usually as a member of a family.	A place of warmth; a place of familiarity; comforting; a place of safety and security. "Home" usually has a positive connotation.
Snake	A long reptile with no limbs and strong jaws that moves along the ground; some snakes have a poisonous bite.	An evil omen; a slithery creature (human or nonhuman) that is deceitful or unwelcome. "Snake" usually has a negative connotation.
Winter	A season of the year that is the coldest, usually from December to February in the northern hemisphere and from June to August in the southern hemisphere.	Circle of life, especially that of death and dying; cold or icy; dark and gloomy; hibernation, sleep, or rest. Winter can have a negative connotation, although many who have access to heat may enjoy the snowy season from their homes.

Analyzing Word Parts

By learning some of the etymologies of words and their parts, readers can break new words down into components and analyze their combined meanings. For example, the root word *soph* is Greek for wise or knowledge. Knowing this informs the meanings of English words including *sophomore, sophisticated,* and *philosophy.* Those who also know that *phil* is Greek for love will realize that *philosophy* means the love of knowledge. They can then extend this knowledge of *phil* to understand *philanthropist* (one who loves people), *bibliophile* (book lover), *philharmonic* (loving harmony), *hydrophilic* (water-loving), and so on. In addition, *phob-* derives from the Greek *phobos,* meaning fear. This informs all words ending with it as meaning fear of various things: *acrophobia* (fear of heights), *arachnophobia* (fear of spiders), *claustrophobia* (fear of enclosed spaces), *ergophobia* (fear of work), *homophobia* (fear of homosexuality), and *hydrophobia* (fear of water), among others.

Some English word origins from other languages, like ancient Greek, are found in large numbers and varieties of English words. An advantage of the shared ancestry of these words is that once readers recognize the meanings of some Greek words or word roots, they can determine or at least get an idea of what many different English words mean. As an example, the Greek word *métron* means to measure, a measure, or something used to measure; the English word meter derives from it. Knowing this informs many other English words, including *altimeter, barometer, diameter, hexameter, isometric,* and *metric.* While readers must know the meanings of the other parts of these words to decipher their meaning fully, they already have an idea that they are all related in some way to measures or measuring.

While all English words ultimately derive from a proto-language known as Indo-European, many of them historically came into the developing English vocabulary later, from sources like the ancient Greeks' language, the Latin used throughout Europe and much of the Middle East during the reign of the Roman Empire, and the Anglo-Saxon languages used by England's early tribes. In addition to classic revivals and native foundations, by the Renaissance era other influences included French, German, Italian, and Spanish. Today we can often discern English word meanings by knowing common roots and affixes, particularly from Greek and Latin.

The following is a list of common prefixes and their meanings:

Prefix	Definition	Examples
a-	without	atheist, agnostic
ad-	to, toward	advance
ante-	before	antecedent, antedate
anti-	opposing	antipathy, antidote
auto-	self	autonomy, autobiography
bene-	well, good	benefit, benefactor
bi-	two	bisect, biennial
bio-	life	biology, biosphere
chron-	time	chronometer, synchronize
circum-	around	circumspect, circumference
com-	with, together	commotion, complicate
contra-	against, opposing	contradict, contravene
cred-	belief, trust	credible, credit
de-	from	depart
dem-	people	demographics, democracy
dis-	away, off, down, not	dissent, disappear
equi-	equal, equally	equivalent
ex-	former, out of	extract
for-	away, off, from	forget, forswear
fore-	before, previous	foretell, forefathers
homo-	same, equal	homogenized
hyper-	excessive, over	hypercritical, hypertension
in-	in, into	intrude, invade
inter-	among, between	intercede, interrupt
mal-	bad, poorly, not	malfunction
micr-	small	microbe, microscope
mis-	bad, poorly, not	misspell, misfire
mono-	one, single	monogamy, monologue
mor-	die, death	mortality, mortuary
neo-	new	neolithic, neoconservative
non-	not	nonentity, nonsense
omni-	all, everywhere	omniscient
over-	above	overbearing
pan-	all, entire	panorama, pandemonium
para-	beside, beyond	parallel, paradox
phil-	love, affection	philosophy, philanthropic
poly-	many	polymorphous, polygamous

Prefix	Definition	Examples
pre-	before, previous	prevent, preclude
prim-	first, early	primitive, primary
pro-	forward, in place of	propel, pronoun
re-	back, backward, again	revoke, recur
sub-	under, beneath	subjugate, substitute
super-	above, extra	supersede, supernumerary
trans-	across, beyond, over	transact, transport
ultra-	beyond, excessively	ultramodern, ultrasonic, ultraviolet
un-	not, reverse of	unhappy, unlock
vis-	to see	visage, visible

The following is a list of common suffixes and their meanings:

Suffix	Definition	Examples
-able	likely, able to	capable, tolerable
-ance	act, condition	acceptance, vigilance
-ard	one that does excessively	drunkard, wizard
-ation	action, state	occupation, starvation
-cy	state, condition	accuracy, captaincy
-er	one who does	teacher
-esce	become, grow, continue	convalesce, acquiesce
-esque	in the style of, like	picturesque, grotesque
-ess	feminine	waitress, lioness
-ful	full of, marked by	thankful, zestful
-ible	able, fit	edible, possible, divisible
-ion	action, result, state	union, fusion
-ish	suggesting, like	churlish, childish
-ism	act, manner, doctrine	barbarism, socialism
-ist	doer, believer	monopolist, socialist
-ition	action, result, state,	sedition, expedition
-ity	quality, condition	acidity, civility
-ize	cause to be, treat with	sterilize, mechanize, criticize
-less	lacking, without	hopeless, countless
-like	like, similar	childlike, dreamlike
-ly	like, of the nature of	friendly, positively
-ment	means, result, action	refreshment, disappointment
-ness	quality, state	greatness, tallness
-or	doer, office, action	juror, elevator, honor
-ous	marked by, given to	religious, riotous
-some	apt to, showing	tiresome, lonesome
-th	act, state, quality	warmth, width
-ty	quality, state	enmity, activity

Analyzing an Author's Word Choice

An author's word choice can also affect the style, tone, and mood of the text. Word choices, grammatical choices, and syntactical choices can help the audience figure out the scope, purpose, and emphasis. These choices—embedded in the words and sentences of the passage (i.e., the "parts")—help paint the intentions and goals of the author (i.e., the "whole"). For instance, if an author is using strong language like *enrage, ignite, infuriate,* and *antagonize,* then they may be cueing the reader into their own rage or they may be trying to incite anger in other. Likewise, if an author is continually using rapid, simple sentences, he or she might be trying to incite excitement and nervousness. These different choices and styles affect the overall message, or purpose. Sometimes the subject matter or audience will be discussed explicitly, but often readers have to decode the passage, or "break it down," to find the target audience and intentions. Meanwhile, the impact of the article can be personal or historical, for example, depending upon the passage—it can either "speak" to you personally or "capture" an historical era.

Analyzing Text Structure

Text structure is the way in which the author organizes and presents textual information so readers can follow and comprehend it. One kind of text structure is sequence. This means the author arranges the text in a logical order from beginning to middle to end. There are three types of sequences:

- Chronological: ordering events in time from earliest to latest

- Spatial: describing objects, people, or spaces according to their relationships to one another in space

- Order of Importance: addressing topics, characters, or ideas according to how important they are, from either least important to most important

Chronological sequence is the most common sequential text structure. Readers can identify sequential structure by looking for words that signal it, like *first, earlier, meanwhile, next, then, later, finally;* and specific times and dates the author includes as chronological references.

Problem-Solution Text Structure
The problem-solution text structure organizes textual information by presenting readers with a problem and then developing its solution throughout the course of the text. The author may present a variety of alternatives as possible solutions, eliminating each as they are found unsuccessful, or gradually leading up to the ultimate solution. For example, in fiction, an author might write a murder mystery novel and have the character(s) solve it through investigating various clues or character alibis until the killer is identified. In nonfiction, an author writing an essay or book on a real-world problem might discuss various alternatives and explain their disadvantages or why they would not work before identifying the best solution. For scientific research, an author reporting and discussing scientific experiment results would explain why various alternatives failed or succeeded.

Comparison-Contrast Text Structure
Comparison identifies similarities between two or more things. **Contrast** identifies differences between two or more things. Authors typically employ both to illustrate relationships between things by highlighting their commonalities and deviations. For example, a writer might compare Windows and Linux as operating systems, and contrast Linux as free and open-source vs. Windows as proprietary. When writing an essay, sometimes it is useful to create an image of the two objects or events you are comparing or contrasting. Venn diagrams are useful because they show the differences as well as the similarities

between two things. Once you've seen the similarities and differences on paper, it might be helpful to create an outline of the essay with both comparison and contrast. Every outline will look different, because every two or more things will have a different number of comparisons and contrasts. Say you are trying to compare and contrast carrots with sweet potatoes. Here is an example of a compare/contrast outline using those topics:

- Introduction: Talk about why you are comparing and contrasting carrots and sweet potatoes. Give the thesis statement.

- Body paragraph 1: Sweet potatoes and carrots are both root vegetables (similarity)

- Body paragraph 2: Sweet potatoes and carrots are both orange (similarity)

- Body paragraph 3: Sweet potatoes and carrots have different nutritional components (difference)

- Conclusion: Restate the purpose of your comparison/contrast essay.

Of course, if there is only one similarity between your topics and two differences, you will want to rearrange your outline. Always tailor your essay to what works best with your topic.

Descriptive Text Structure
Description can be both a type of text structure and a type of text. Some texts are descriptive throughout entire books. For example, a book may describe the geography of a certain country, state, or region, or tell readers all about dolphins by describing many of their characteristics. Many other texts are not descriptive throughout, but use descriptive passages within the overall text. The following are a few examples of descriptive text:

- When the author describes a character in a novel
- When the author sets the scene for an event by describing the setting
- When a biographer describes the personality and behaviors of a real-life individual
- When a historian describes the details of a particular battle within a book about a specific war
- When a travel writer describes the climate, people, foods, and/or customs of a certain place

A hallmark of description is using sensory details, painting a vivid picture so readers can imagine it almost as if they were experiencing it personally.

Cause and Effect Text Structure
When using cause and effect to extrapolate meaning from text, readers must determine the cause when the author only communicates effects. For example, if a description of a child eating an ice cream cone includes details like beads of sweat forming on the child's face and the ice cream dripping down her hand faster than she can lick it off, the reader can infer or conclude it must be hot outside. A useful technique for making such decisions is wording them in "If...then" form, e.g. "If the child is perspiring and the ice cream melting, it may be a hot day." Cause and effect text structures explain why certain events or actions resulted in particular outcomes. For example, an author might describe America's historical large flocks of dodo birds, the fact that gunshots did not startle/frighten dodos, and that because dodos did not flee, settlers killed whole flocks in one hunting session, explaining how the dodo was hunted into extinction.

Understanding Authorial Purpose and Perspective

Authors may have many purposes for writing a specific text. Their purposes may be to try and convince readers to agree with their position on a subject, to impart information, or to entertain. Other writers are motivated to write from a desire to express their own feelings. Authors' purposes are their reasons for writing something. A single author may have one overriding purpose for writing or multiple reasons. An author may explicitly state their intention in the text, or the reader may need to infer that intention. Those who read reflectively benefit from identifying the purpose because it enables them to analyze information in the text. By knowing why the author wrote the text, readers can glean ideas for how to approach it. The following is a list of questions readers can ask in order to discern an author's purpose for writing a text:

- From the title of the text, why do you think the author wrote it?
- Was the purpose of the text to give information to readers?
- Did the author want to describe an event, issue, or individual?
- Was it written to express emotions and thoughts?
- Did the author want to convince readers to consider a particular issue?
- Was the author primarily motivated to write the text to entertain?
- Why do you think the author wrote this text from a certain point of view?
- What is your response to the text as a reader?
- Did the author state their purpose for writing it?

Readers should read to interpret information rather than simply content themselves with roles as text consumers. Being able to identify an author's purpose efficiently improves reading comprehension, develops critical thinking, and makes readers more likely to consider issues in depth before accepting writer viewpoints. Authors of fiction frequently write to entertain readers. Another purpose for writing fiction is making a political statement; for example, Jonathan Swift wrote "A Modest Proposal" (1729) as a political satire. Another purpose for writing fiction as well as nonfiction is to persuade readers to take some action or further a particular cause. Fiction authors and poets both frequently write to evoke certain moods; for example, Edgar Allan Poe wrote novels, short stories, and poems that evoke moods of gloom, guilt, terror, and dread. Another purpose of poets is evoking certain emotions: love is popular, as in Shakespeare's sonnets and numerous others. In "The Waste Land" (1922), T.S. Eliot evokes society's alienation, disaffection, sterility, and fragmentation.

Authors seldom directly state their purposes in texts. Some readers may be confronted with nonfiction texts such as biographies, histories, magazine and newspaper articles, and instruction manuals, among others. To identify the purpose in nonfiction texts, students can ask the following questions:

- Is the author trying to teach something?
- Is the author trying to persuade the reader?
- Is the author imparting factual information only?
- Is this a reliable source?
- Does the author have some kind of hidden agenda?

To apply author purpose in nonfictional passages, readers can also analyze sentence structure, word choice, and transitions to answer the aforementioned questions and to make inferences. For example, authors wanting to convince readers to view a topic negatively often choose words with negative connotations.

Narrative Writing

Narrative writing tells a story. The most prominent examples of narrative writing are fictional novels. Here are some examples:

- Mark Twain's The Adventures of Tom Sawyer and The Adventures of Huckleberry Finn
- Victor Hugo's *Les Misérables*
- Charles Dickens' Great Expectations, David Copperfield, and A Tale of Two Cities
- Jane Austen's Northanger Abbey, Mansfield Park, Pride and Prejudice, and Sense and Sensibility
- Toni Morrison's Beloved, The Bluest Eye, and Song of Solomon
- Gabriel García Márquez's One Hundred Years of Solitude and Love in the Time of Cholera

Some nonfiction works are also written in narrative form. For example, some authors choose a narrative style to convey factual information about a topic, such as a specific animal, country, geographic region, and scientific or natural phenomenon.

Since narrative is the type of writing that tells a story, it must be told by someone, who is the narrator. The narrator may be a fictional character telling the story from their own viewpoint. This narrator uses the first person (*I, me, my, mine* and *we, us, our,* and *ours*). The narrator may simply be the author; for example, when Louisa May Alcott writes "Dear reader" in *Little Women*, she (the author) addresses us as readers. In this case, the novel is typically told in third person, referring to the characters as he, she, they, or them. Another more common technique is the omniscient narrator; i.e. the story is told by an unidentified individual who sees and knows everything about the events and characters—not only their externalized actions, but also their internalized feelings and thoughts. Second person, i.e. writing the story by addressing readers as "you" throughout, is less frequently used.

Expository Writing

Expository writing is also known as informational writing. Its purpose is not to tell a story as in narrative writing, to paint a picture as in descriptive writing, or to persuade readers to agree with something as in argumentative writing. Rather, its point is to communicate information to the reader. As such, the point of view of the author will necessarily be more objective. Whereas other types of writing appeal to the reader's emotions, appeal to the reader's reason by using logic, or use subjective descriptions to sway the reader's opinion or thinking, expository writing seeks to do none of these but simply to provide facts, evidence, observations, and objective descriptions of the subject matter. Some examples of expository writing include research reports, journal articles, articles and books about historical events or periods, academic subject textbooks, news articles and other factual journalistic reports, essays, how-to articles, and user instruction manuals.

Technical Writing

Technical writing is similar to expository writing in that it is factual, objective, and intended to provide information to the reader. Indeed, it may even be considered a subcategory of expository writing. However, technical writing differs from expository writing in that (1) it is specific to a particular field, discipline, or subject; and (2) it uses the specific technical terminology that belongs only to that area. Writing that uses technical terms is intended only for an audience familiar with those terms. A primary example of technical writing today is writing related to computer programming and use.

Persuasive Writing

Persuasive writing is intended to persuade the reader to agree with the author's position. It is also known as argumentative writing. Some writers may be responding to other writers' arguments, in which case they make reference to those authors or text and then disagree with them. However, another common technique is for the author to anticipate opposing viewpoints in general, both from other authors and from the author's own readers. The author brings up these opposing viewpoints, and then refutes them before they can even be raised, strengthening the author's argument. Writers persuade readers by appealing to their reason, which Aristotle called *logos;* appealing to emotion, which Aristotle called *pathos;* or appealing to readers based on the author's character and credibility, which Aristotle called *ethos.*

Analyzing Characters' Points of View

In fiction, authors either write from the first-, second-, or third-person point of view. Throughout a literary work, authors may choose to write exclusively from one point of view, two points of view, or even all three. Analyzing points of view often leads readers to reflect and consider various perspectives on a given subject.

First Person
First-person singular point of view becomes apparent when the author uses the pronouns "I," "me," "my," and "mine." The use of pronouns "we," "us," "our," and "ours" indicates the use of the first-person plural. Authors often choose first-person point of view to develop a close connection with the audience. First-person point of view brings a familiar and human feel to the writing, to which many readers relate. Often filled with subjective messaging, first-person point of view strives to connect with the readers on a personal level. Consider the following first-person point of view:

> "It was Sunday, the best day of the week. After church, Mama would take me straight to Grandma's house for cookies and tea. We would rock on the rocking chair on the front porch as if we didn't have a care in the world—truth be told, we really didn't have a care in the world."

This example demonstrates a clear example of how an author strives to pull in the reader with the use of first-person point of view. Readers connect to the sentimentality and develop a sense of nostalgia.

Second Person
Second-person point of view employs the pronouns "you," "your," and "yours." Only occasionally used in fiction, second-person point of view requires a lot more effort to develop. When authors want to fully immerse their audience in the experiences unfolding in the story, or when they wish for the audience to imagine themselves in that exact place and time, feeling that exact way, they may choose a second-person point of view. Consider the following passage:

> "Imagine you were at the site when the first thunderbolt fell from the sky. You look up and cannot believe your eyes. At first, you are mesmerized, but that feeling quickly morphs into shock. You look to your left, then to your right, because in that moment, you do not want to be alone. You want nothing more than to share these sensations with someone you love."

Second-person point of view, however, is difficult to sustain for a long period of time, especially in fiction, and it is better used for only brief moments when authors wish to plunge their audience directly into the storyline.

Third Person

When written from the third-person point of view, the writing can sometimes feel distant. The reader is somewhat removed from the experiences taking place. In literature, third-person points of view are developed with the use of a narrator who acts as a person on the outside looking in and giving play-by-play accounts of what is taking place. Pronouns "he," "she," "they," and even "it" can be used to describe the scenes in the story. Consider the following passage:

> "Emily knew it was just a matter of time before she would have to leave. She heard the clock ticking in the big, empty hallway, and it seemed as loud as a thousand church bells. She sat—completely still—until the clock struck twelve. Then she drew a deep breath, stood, picked up her bags, and left. 'Soon, it will all be over', she whispered to herself."

Although the narrator is describing Emily from a distance, and readers also feel somewhat removed, they can still feel that sense of fear, or perhaps anxiety, as Emily awaits the moment when she must leave.

Analyzing point of view is an essential skill for readers to develop in order to gain a deeper understanding of the storyline, as well as the different characters who all play a role in the story's development.

Interpreting Authorial Decisions Rhetorically

One of the freedoms in reading is to derive a unique perspective on the author's intent. Writing is an art form and can have many different interpretations. Often, readers who read the same literary work may have varying opinions regarding the author's intent. In fact, their varying interpretations might also differ from the author's intended message. Reading literature is less about being right than about striving to derive meaning from the message. The beauty of literature, as in any art form, is that it is open to interpretation.

There have been many theories about the intended meaning of Lewis Carroll's *Alice's Adventures in Wonderland*, from a bizarre take on the world brought on by drug use, to an obsession with food and drink—and many other interpretations as well. However, the author himself said that the intent was nothing more than to entertain a child friend by creating a dreamlike, fantastical tale. Does that mean, then, that readers should stop imagining, should stop analyzing, and should simply accept the author's intended meaning? Although it should be respected, the author's intended meaning may not be the only interpretation. Literature can often take on a life of its own, and each reader is free to interpret literature in their own unique way, while keeping an open mind on other perspectives, particularly that of the author. Authors may learn a great deal about their work of art through the eyes of their readers, and authors may develop different perspectives based on their readers' keen observations and discoveries. True artists appreciate different interpretations of their work of art, and they regard the varied interpretations as something to be celebrated. Readers and authors affect one another, learn from one another, and become more skilled in their art when they allow their own interpretations to be analyzed.

Differentiating Between Various Perspectives

"Point of view" refers to the type of narration the author employs in a given story. "Perspective" refers to how characters perceive what is happening within the story. The characters' perspectives reveal their attitudes and help to shape their unique personalities. Consider the following scenario:

> "The family grabbed their snacks and blankets, loaded up the van, and headed out to the neighborhood park, even though Suki would have preferred to stay home. Once they settled in at their spot on the grass, the celebration was about to start. Within minutes, the fireworks began—crack, bang, pop! Hendrix jumped up and down with glee, Suki angrily put down her phone, and the dog yelped and buried its head under the blankets."

Each character was experiencing the same event—fireworks—and yet each character had a different reaction. Hendrix seems excited, Suki, angry, and the dog, frightened. No *one* perspective is the "right" perspective, just as no particular perspective is wrong; they are simply perspectives. What makes characters unique within a story are their unique perspectives. When authors develop characters with unique personalities and differing perspectives, stories are not only more believable, but they are more alive, more colorful, and more interesting. If all characters had the same one-dimensional perspective, the story would likely be quite dull. There would never be a protagonist or antagonist, and there would be no reason to examine why each character acts and reacts to situations in such unique ways. Differentiating between various perspectives in a story can also lead to a much deeper understanding. For instance, it seems relatively easy to consider the perspective of the protagonist in any story since most readers connect with good and reject evil. But readers might wish to explore the story through the eyes of the antagonist. They might want to discover how the antagonist ended up so villainous, what events led to their corruption, and what, if anything, might lead them back to truth and justice.

Perspectives are how individuals see the world in which they live, and they are often formed from the individual's unique life experiences, their morals, and their values. Differentiating between various perspectives in literature helps readers to develop a greater appreciation for the story and for each character that helps to shape that story.

Comparing Different Sources of Information

Identifying Specific Information from a Printed Communication
Business Memos
Whereas everyday office memos were traditionally typed on paper, photocopied, and distributed, today they are more often typed on computers and distributed via e-mail, both interoffice and externally. Technology has thus made these communications more immediate. It is also helpful for people to read carefully and be familiar with memo components. For example, e-mails automatically provide the same "To:, From:, and Re:" lines traditionally required in paper memos, and in corresponding places—the top of the page/screen. Readers should observe whether "To: names/positions" include all intended recipients in case of misdirection errors or omitted recipients. "From:" informs sender level, role, and who will receive responses when people click "Reply." Users must be careful not to click "Reply All" unintentionally. They should also observe the "CC:" line, typically below "Re:," showing additional recipients.

Classified Ads

Classified advertisements include "Help Wanted" ads informing readers of positions open for hiring, real estate listings, cars for sale, and home and business services available. Traditional ads in newspapers had to save space, and this necessity has largely transferred to online ads. Because of needing to save space, advertisers employ many abbreviations. For example, here are some examples of abbreviations:

- FT=full-time
- PT=part-time
- A/P=accounts payable
- A/R=accounts receivable
- Asst.=assistant
- Bkkg.=bookkeeping
- Comm.=commission
- Bet.=between
- EOE=equal opportunity employer
- G/L=general ledger
- Immed.=immediately
- Exc.=excellent
- Exp.=experience
- Eves.=evenings
- Secy.=secretary
- Temp=temporary
- Sal=salary
- Req=required
- Refs=references
- Wk=week or work
- WPM=words per minute

Classified ads frequently use abbreviations to take up less space, both on paper and digitally on websites. Those who read these ads will find it less confusing if they learn some common abbreviations used by businesses when advertising job positions. Here are some examples:

- Mgt.=management
- Mgr.=manager
- Mfg.=manufacturing
- Nat'l=national
- Dept.=department
- Min.=minimum
- Yrs.=years
- Nec=necessary
- Neg=negotiable
- Oppty=opportunity
- O/T=overtime
- K=1,000

Readers of classified ads may focus on certain features to the exclusion of others. For example, if a reader sees the job title or salary they are seeking, or notices the experience, education, degree, or other credentials required match their own qualifications perfectly, they may fail to notice other important information, like "No benefits." This is important because the employers are disclosing that they will not provide health insurance, retirement accounts, paid sick leave, paid maternity/paternity leave, paid vacation, etc. to any employee whom they hire. Someone expecting a traditional 9 to 5 job who fails to observe that an ad states "Evenings" or just the abbreviation "Eves" will be disappointed, as will the applicant who overlooks a line saying "Some evenings and weekends reqd." Applicants overlooking information like "Apply in person" may e-mail or mail their resumes and receive no response. The job hopeful with no previous experience and one reference must attend to information like "Minimum 5 yrs. exp, 3 refs," meaning they likely will not qualify.

Employment Ads
Job applicants should pay attention to the information included in classified employment ads. On one hand, they do need to believe and accept certain statements, such as "Please, no phone calls," which is frequently used by employers posting ads on Craigslist and similar websites. New applicants just graduated from or still in college will be glad to see "No exp necessary" in some ads, indicating they need no previous work experience in that job category. "FT/PT" means the employer offers the options of working full-time or part-time, another plus for students. On the other hand, ad readers should also take into consideration the fact that many employers list all the attributes of their *ideal* employee, but they do not necessarily expect to find such a candidate. If a potential applicant's education, training, credentials, and experience are not exactly the same as what the employer lists as desired but are not radically different either, it can be productive to apply anyway, while honestly representing one's actual qualifications.

Atlases
A road atlas is a publication designed to assist travelers who are driving on road trips rather than taking airplanes, trains, ships, etc. Travelers use road atlases to determine which routes to take and places to stop; how to navigate specific cities, locate landmarks, estimate mileages and travel times; see photographs of places they plan to visit; and find other travel-related information. One familiar, reputable road atlas is published by the National Geographic Society. It includes detailed, accurate maps of the United States, Canada, and Mexico; historic sites, scenic routes, recreation information, and points of interest; and its Adventure Edition spotlights 100 top U.S. adventure destinations and most popular national parks. The best-selling road atlas in the United States, also probably the best-known and most trusted, is published annually by Rand McNally, which has published road atlases for many years. It includes maps, mileage charts, information on tourism and road construction, maps of individual city details, and the editor's favorite road trips (in the 2016 edition) including recommended points of interest en route.

Owners' Manuals
An owner's manual is typically a booklet, but may also be as short as a page or as long as a book, depending on the individual instance. The purpose of an owner's manual is to give the owner instructions, usually step-by-step, for how to use a specific product or a group or range of products. Manuals accompany consumer products as diverse as cars, computers, tablets, smartphones, printers, home appliances, shop machines, and many others. In addition to directions for operating products, they include important warnings of things *not* to do that pose safety or health hazards or can damage the product and void the manufacturer's product warranty, like immersion in water, exposure to high temperatures, operating something for too long, dropping fragile items, or rough handling. Manuals teach correct operating practices, sequences, precautions, and cautions, averting many costly and/or dangerous mishaps.

Food Labels

When reading the labels on food products, it is often necessary to interpret the nutrition facts and other product information. Without the consumer's being aware and informed of this, much of this information can be very misleading. For example, a popular brand name of corn chips lists the calories, fat, etc. per serving in the nutrition facts printed on the bag, but on closer inspection, it defines a serving size as six chips—far fewer than most people would consume at a time. Serving sizes and the number of servings per container can be unrealistic. For example, a jumbo muffin's wrapper indicates it contains three servings. Not only do most consumers not divide a muffin and eat only part; but it is moreover rather difficult to cut a muffin into equal thirds. A king-sized package of chili cheese-flavored corn chips says it contains 4.5 servings per container. This is not very useful information, since people cannot divide the package into equal servings and are unlikely to eat four servings and then ½ a serving.

Product Packaging

Consumers today cannot take product labels at face value. While many people do not read or even look at the information on packages before eating their contents, those who do must use more consideration and analysis than they might expect to understand it. For example, a well-known brand of strawberry-flavored breakfast toaster pastry displays a picture of four whole strawberries on the wrapper. While this looks appealing, encouraging consumers to infer the product contains wholesome fruit—and perhaps even believe it contains four whole strawberries—reading the ingredients list reveals it contains only 2 percent or less of dried strawberries. A consumer must be detail-oriented (and curious or motivated enough) to read the full ingredients list, which also reveals unhealthy corn syrup and high fructose corn syrup high on the list after enriched flour. Consumers must also educate themselves about euphemistically misleading terms: "enriched" flour has vitamins and minerals added, but it is refined flour without whole grain, bran, or fiber.

While manufacturers generally provide extensive information printed on their package labels, it is typically in very small print—many consumers do not read it—and even consumers who do read all the information must look for small details to discover that the information is often not realistic. For example, a box of brownie mix lists grams of fat, total calories, and calories from fat. However, by paying attention to small details like asterisks next to this information, and finding the additional information referenced by the asterisks, the consumer discovers that these amounts are for only the dry mix—not the added eggs, oil, or milk. Consumers typically do not eat dry cake mixes, and having to determine and add the fat and calories from the additional ingredients is inconvenient. In another example, a box of macaroni and cheese mix has an asterisk by the fat grams indicating these are for the macaroni only without the cheese, butter, or milk required, which contributes 6.4 times more fat.

Ingredients' Lists

Consumers can realize the importance of reading drug labeling through an analogy: What might occur if they were to read only part of the directions on a standardized test? Reading only part of the directions on medications can have similar, even more serious consequences. Prescription drug packages typically contain inserts, which provide extremely extensive, thorough, detailed information, including results of clinical trials and statistics showing patient responses and adverse effects. Some over-the-counter medications include inserts, and some do not. "Active ingredients" are those ingredients making medication effective. "Inactive ingredients" including flavorings, preservatives, stabilizers, and emulsifiers have purposes, but not to treat symptoms. "Uses" indicates which symptoms a medication is meant to treat. "Directions" tell the dosage, frequency, maximum daily amount, and other requirements, like "Take with food," "Do not operate heavy machinery while using," etc. Drug labels also state how to store the product, like at what temperature or away from direct sunlight or humidity.

Many drugs which were previously available only by doctor prescription have recently become available over the counter without a prescription. While enough years of testing may have determined that these substances typically do not cause serious problems, consumers must nevertheless thoroughly read and understand all the information on the labels before taking them. If they do not, they could still suffer serious harm. For example, some individuals have allergies to specific substances. Both prescription and over-the-counter medication products list their ingredients, including warnings about allergies. Allergic reactions can include anaphylactic shock, which can be fatal if not treated immediately. Also, consumers must read and follow dosing directions: taking more than directed can cause harm, and taking less can be ineffective to treat symptoms. Some medication labels warn not to mix them with certain other drugs to avoid harmful drug interactions. Additionally, without reading ingredients, some consumers take multiple products including the same active ingredients, resulting in overdoses.

Identifying Information from a Graphic Representation of Information
Line Graphs
Line graphs are useful for visually representing data that vary continuously over time, like an individual student's test scores. The horizontal or x-axis shows dates/times; the vertical or y-axis shows point values. A dot is plotted on the point where each horizontal date line intersects each vertical number line, and then these dots are connected, forming a line. Line graphs show whether changes in values over time exhibit trends like ascending, descending, flat, or more variable, like going up and down at different times. For example, suppose a student's scores on the same type of reading test were 75% in October, 80% in November, 78% in December, 82% in January, 85% in February, 88% in March, and 90% in April. A line graph of these scores would look like this:

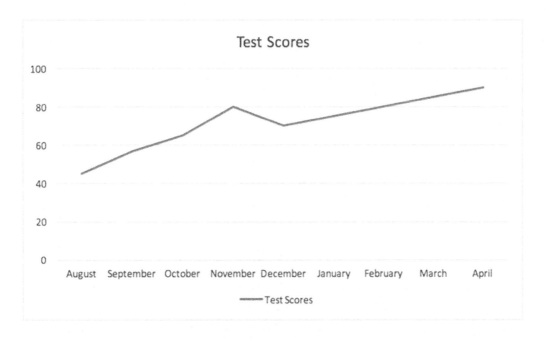

Bar Graphs
Bar graphs feature equally spaced, horizontal or vertical rectangular bars representing numerical values. They can show change over time as line graphs do, but unlike line graphs, bar graphs can also show differences and similarities among values at a single point in time. Bar graphs are also helpful for visually representing data from different categories, especially when the horizontal axis displays some value that is

not numerical, like various countries with inches of annual rainfall. The following is a bar graph that compares different classes and how many books they read:

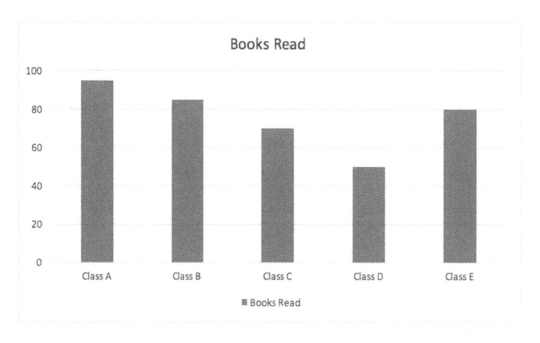

Pie Charts

Pie charts, also called circle graphs, are good for representing percentages or proportions of a whole quantity because they represent the whole as a circle or "pie," with the various proportion values shown as "slices" or wedges of the pie. This gives viewers a clear idea of how much of a total each item occupies. To calculate central angles to make each portion the correct size, multiply each percentage by 3.6 (= 360/100). For example, biologists may have information that 60% of Americans have brown eyes, 20% have hazel eyes, 15% have blue eyes, and 5% have green eyes. A pie chart of these distributions would look like this:

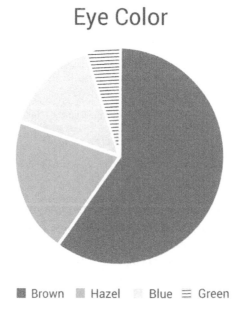

Line Plots

Rather than showing trends or changes over time like line graphs, line plots show the frequency with which a value occurs in a group. Line plots are used for visually representing data sets that total 50 or fewer values. They make visible features like gaps between some data points, clusters of certain numbers/number ranges, and outliers (data points with significantly smaller or larger values than others). For example, the age ranges in a class of nursing students might appear like this in a line plot:

XXXXXXXXX	XXXXX	XX	X	XXX	XX	X
18	23	28	33	38	43	48

Pictograms

Magazines, newspapers, and other similar publications designed for consumption by the general public often use pictograms to represent data. Pictograms feature icons or symbols that look like whatever category of data is being counted, like little silhouettes shaped like human beings commonly used to represent people. If the data involve large numbers, like populations, one person symbol might represent one million people, or one thousand, etc. For smaller values, such as how many individuals out of ten fit a given description, one symbol might equal one person. Male and female silhouettes are used to differentiate gender, and child shapes for children. Little clock symbols are used to represent amounts of time, such as a given number of hours; calendar pages might depict months; suns and moons could show days and nights; hourglasses might represent minutes. While pictogram symbols are easily recognizable and appealing to general viewers, one disadvantage is that it is difficult to display partial symbols for in-between quantities.

Integration of Knowledge and Ideas

Understanding Authors' Claims

In academic writing, an author's claim refers to the argument being made, the main idea, or the thesis statement. It is the point that the author chooses to impress upon the audience whether that point is a truth that can be proven or an opinion that can be supported. In order for claims to be valid, they should always be accompanied by supporting evidence. To understand an author's claim, readers first identify the claim and then look for the supporting evidence. Finally, they analyze the evidence to determine its strength. Is the evidence based on popular belief, expert opinion, or empirical data?

But understanding an author's claim isn't just about identifying the main argument. It is also about considering how the author supports that claim and ruling out any bias that would weaken the argument. Is the author trying to share findings, or is the intent more about persuasion? Even if the author's intent is to persuade, the argument can still be valid. After all, a well-supported claim that addiction to drugs and alcohol negatively affects a person's social, emotional, and physical wellbeing might be persuasive, and it is certainly a valid claim. The three modes of persuasion involve:

- Ethos, which refers to the author's credibility or character
- Pathos, which refers to emotion
- Logos, which refers to logic

Examining the mode the author uses results in a greater understanding of the author's claims, enabling the reader to determine the claim's credibility. To further understand the author's claim, it also helps to identify the author's intended audience. Is the author writing directly to scholars or to students? Is the message intended to effect governmental or social change?

Authors present their claim and strive to support it with reasons and evidence. It is the reader's responsibility to identify the claim and the supporting evidence, and to evaluate whether the supporting evidence is strong enough to hold up the author's claim.

Differentiating Between Facts and Opinions

Facts and Opinions

A **fact** is a statement that is true empirically or an event that has actually occurred in reality, and can be proven or supported by evidence; it is generally objective. In contrast, an **opinion** is subjective, representing something that someone believes rather than something that exists in the absolute. People's individual understandings, feelings, and perspectives contribute to variations in opinion. Though facts are typically objective in nature, in some instances, a statement of fact may be both factual and yet also subjective. For example, emotions are individual subjective experiences. If an individual says that they feel happy or sad, the feeling is subjective, but the statement is factual; hence, it is a subjective fact. In contrast, if one person tells another that the other is feeling happy or sad—whether this is true or not—that is an assumption or an opinion.

Biases

Biases usually occur when someone allows their personal preferences or ideologies to interfere with what should be an objective decision. In personal situations, someone is biased towards someone if they favor them in an unfair way. In academic writing, being biased in your sources means leaving out objective information that would turn the argument one way or the other. The evidence of bias in academic writing makes the text less credible, so be sure to present all viewpoints when writing, not just your own, so to avoid coming off as biased. Being objective when presenting information or dealing with people usually allows the person to gain more credibility.

Stereotypes

Stereotypes are preconceived notions that place a particular rule or characteristics on an entire group of people. Stereotypes are usually offensive to the group they refer to or allies of that group, and often have negative connotations. The reinforcement of stereotypes isn't always obvious. Sometimes stereotypes can be very subtle and are still widely used in order for people to understand categories within the world. For example, saying that women are more emotional and intuitive than men is a stereotype, although this is still an assumption used by many in order to understand the differences between one another.

Using Evidence to Make Connections Between Different Texts That are Related by Topic

Comparing and Contrasting Themes from Print and Other Sources

The **theme** of a piece of text is the central idea the author communicates. Whereas the topic of a passage of text may be concrete in nature, by contrast the theme is always conceptual. For example, while the topic of Mark Twain's novel *The Adventures of Huckleberry Finn* might be described as something like the coming-of-age experiences of a poor, illiterate, functionally orphaned boy around and on the Mississippi River in 19th-century Missouri, one theme of the book might be that human beings are corrupted by society. Another might be that slavery and "civilized" society itself are hypocritical. Whereas the main idea in a text is the most important single point that the author wants to make, the theme is the concept or view around which the author centers the text.

Throughout time, humans have told stories with similar themes. Some themes are universal across time, space, and culture. These include themes of the individual as a hero, conflicts of the individual against nature, the individual against society, change vs. tradition, the circle of life, coming-of-age, and the complexities of love. Themes involving war and peace have featured prominently in diverse works, like Homer's *Iliad*, Tolstoy's *War and Peace* (1869), Stephen Crane's *The Red Badge of Courage* (1895), Hemingway's *A Farewell to Arms* (1929), and Margaret Mitchell's *Gone with the Wind* (1936). Another universal literary theme is that of the quest. These appear in folklore from countries and cultures worldwide, including the Gilgamesh Epic, Arthurian legend's Holy Grail quest, Virgil's *Aeneid*, Homer's *Odyssey*, and the *Argonautica*. Cervantes' *Don Quixote* is a parody of chivalric quests. J.R.R. Tolkien's *The Lord of the Rings* trilogy (1954) also features a quest.

One instance of similar themes across cultures is when those cultures are in countries that are geographically close to each other. For example, a folklore story of a rabbit in the moon using a mortar and pestle is shared among China, Japan, Korea, and Thailand—making medicine in China, making rice cakes in Japan and Korea, and hulling rice in Thailand. Another instance is when cultures are more distant geographically, but their languages are related. For example, East Turkestan's Uighurs and people in Turkey share tales of folk hero Effendi Nasreddin Hodja. Another instance, which may either be called cultural diffusion or simply reflect commonalities in the human imagination, involves shared themes among geographically and linguistically different cultures: both Cameroon's and Greece's folklore tell of centaurs; Cameroon, India, Malaysia, Thailand, and Japan, of mermaids; Brazil, Peru, China, Japan, Malaysia, Indonesia, and Cameroon, of underwater civilizations; and China, Japan, Thailand, Vietnam, Malaysia, Brazil, and Peru, of shape-shifters.

Two prevalent literary themes are love and friendship, which can end happily, sadly, or both. William Shakespeare's *Romeo and Juliet*, Emily Brontë's *Wuthering Heights*, Leo Tolstoy's *Anna Karenina*, and both *Pride and Prejudice* and *Sense and Sensibility* by Jane Austen are famous examples. Another theme recurring in popular literature is of revenge, an old theme in dramatic literature, e.g. Elizabethans Thomas Kyd's *The Spanish Tragedy* and Thomas Middleton's *The Revenger's Tragedy*. Some more well-known instances include Shakespeare's tragedies *Hamlet* and *Macbeth*, Alexandre Dumas' *The Count of Monte Cristo*, John Grisham's *A Time to Kill*, and Stieg Larsson's *The Girl Who Kicked the Hornet's Nest*.

Themes are underlying meanings in literature. For example, if a story's main idea is a character succeeding against all odds, the theme is overcoming obstacles. If a story's main idea is one character wanting what another character has, the theme is jealousy. If a story's main idea is a character doing something they were afraid to do, the theme is courage. Themes differ from topics in that a topic is a subject matter; a theme is the author's opinion about it. For example, a work could have a topic of war and a theme that war is a curse. Authors present themes through characters' feelings, thoughts, experiences, dialogue, plot actions, and events. Themes function as "glue" holding other essential story elements together. They offer readers insights into characters' experiences, the author's philosophy, and how the world works.

Using Text Features
Table of Contents and Index
When examining a book, a journal article, a monograph, or other publication, the table of contents is in the front. In books, it is typically found following the title page, publication information (often on the facing side of the title page), and dedication page, when one is included. In shorter publications, the table of contents may follow the title page, or the title on the same page. The table of contents in a book lists the number and title of each chapter and its beginning page number. An index, which is most common in books but may also be included in shorter works, is at the back of the publication. Books, especially academic texts, frequently have two: a subject index and an author index. Readers can look alphabetically

for specific subjects in the subject index. Likewise, they can look up specific authors cited, quoted, discussed, or mentioned in the author index.

The index in a book offers particular advantages to students. For example, college course instructors typically assign certain textbooks, but do not expect students to read the entire book from cover to cover immediately. They usually assign specific chapters to read in preparation for specific lectures and/or discussions in certain upcoming classes. Reading portions at a time, some students may find references they either do not fully understand or want to know more about. They can look these topics up in the book's subject index to find them in later chapters. When a text author refers to another author, students can also look up the name in the book's author index to find all page numbers of all other references to that author. College students also typically are assigned research papers to write. A book's subject and author indexes can guide students to pages that may help inform them of other books to use for researching paper topics.

Headings

Headings and subheadings concisely inform readers what each section of a paper contains, as well as showing how its information is organized both visually and verbally. Headings are typically up to about five words long. They are not meant to give in-depth analytical information about the topic of their section, but rather an idea of its subject matter. Text authors should maintain consistent style across all headings. Readers should not expect headings if there is not material for more than one heading at each level, just as a list is unnecessary for a single item. Subheadings may be a bit longer than headings because they expand upon them. Readers should skim the subheadings in a paper to use them as a map of how content is arranged. Subheadings are in smaller fonts than headings to mirror relative importance. Subheadings are not necessary for every paragraph. They should enhance content, not substitute for topic sentences.

When a heading is brief, simple, and written in the form of a question, it can have the effect of further drawing readers into the text. An effective author will also answer the question in the heading soon in the following text. Question headings and their text answers are particularly helpful for engaging readers with average reading skills. Both headings and subheadings are most effective with more readers when they are obvious, simple, and get to their points immediately. Simple headings attract readers; simple subheadings allow readers a break, during which they also inform reader decisions whether to continue reading or not. Headings stand out from other text through boldface, but also italicizing and underlining them would be excessive. Uppercase-lowercase headings are easier for readers to comprehend than all capitals. More legible fonts are better. Some experts prefer serif fonts in text, but sans-serif fonts in headings. Brief subheadings that preview upcoming chunks of information reach more readers.

Text Features

Textbooks that are designed well employ varied text features for organizing their main ideas, illustrating central concepts, spotlighting significant details, and signaling evidence that supports the ideas and points conveyed. When a textbook uses these features in recurrent patterns that are predictable, it makes it easier for readers to locate information and come up with connections. When readers comprehend how to make use of text features, they will take less time and effort deciphering how the text is organized, leaving them more time and energy for focusing on the actual content in the text. Instructional activities can include not only previewing text through observing main text features, but moreover through examining and deconstructing the text and ascertaining how the text features can aid them in locating and applying text information for learning.

Included among various text features are a table of contents, headings, subheadings, an index, a glossary, a foreword, a preface, paragraphing spaces, bullet lists, footnotes, sidebars, diagrams, graphs, charts, pictures, illustrations, captions, italics, boldface, colors, and symbols. A glossary is a list of key vocabulary words and/or technical terminology and definitions. This helps readers recognize or learn specialized terms used in the text before reading it. A foreword is typically written by someone other than the text author and appears at the beginning to introduce, inform, recommend, and/or praise the work. A preface is often written by the author and also appears at the beginning, to introduce or explain something about the text, like new additions. A sidebar is a box with text and sometimes graphics at the left or right side of a page, typically focusing on a more specific issue, example, or aspect of the subject. Footnotes are additional comments/notes at the bottom of the page, signaled by superscript numbers in the text.

Text Features on Websites

On the Internet or in computer software programs, text features include URLs, home pages, pop-up menus, drop-down menus, bookmarks, buttons, links, navigation bars, text boxes, arrows, symbols, colors, graphics, logos, and abbreviations. URLs (Universal Resource Locators) indicate the internet "address" or location of a website or web page. They often start with www. (world wide web) or http:// (hypertext transfer protocol) or https:// (the "s" indicates a secure site) and appear in the Internet browser's top address bar. Clickable buttons are often links to specific pages on a website or other external sites. Users can click on some buttons to open pop-up or drop-down menus, which offer a list of actions or departments from which to select. Bookmarks are the electronic versions of physical bookmarks. When users bookmark a website/page, a link is established to the site URL and saved, enabling returning to the site in the future without having to remember its name or URL by clicking the bookmark.

Readers can more easily navigate websites and read their information by observing and utilizing their various text features. For example, most fully developed websites include search bars, where users can type in topics, questions, titles, or names to locate specific information within the large amounts stored on many sites. Navigation bars (software developers frequently use the abbreviation term "navbar") are graphical user interfaces (GUIs) that facilitate visiting different sections, departments, or pages within a website, which can be difficult or impossible to find without these. Typically, they appear as a series of links running horizontally across the top of each page. Navigation bars displayed vertically along the left side of the page are also called sidebars. Links, i.e. hyperlinks, enable hyperspeed browsing by allowing readers to jump to new pages/sites. They may be URLs, words, phrases, images, buttons, etc. They are often but not always underlined and/or blue, or other colors.

Analyzing How Authors Construct Arguments

When authors write text for the purpose of persuading others to agree with them, they assume a position with the subject matter about which they are writing. Rather than presenting information objectively, the author treats the subject matter subjectively so that the information presented supports his or her position. In their argumentation, the author presents information that refutes or weakens opposing positions. Another technique authors use in persuasive writing is to anticipate arguments against the position. When students learn to read subjectively, they gain experience with the concept of persuasion in writing, and learn to identify positions taken by authors. This enhances their reading comprehension and develops their skills for identifying pro and con arguments and biases.

There are five main parts of the classical argument that writers employ in a well-designed stance:

- Introduction: In the introduction to a classical argument, the author establishes goodwill and rapport with the reading audience, warms up the readers, and states the thesis or general theme of the argument.

- Narration: In the narration portion, the author gives a summary of pertinent background information, informs the readers of anything they need to know regarding the circumstances and environment surrounding and/or stimulating the argument, and establishes what is at risk or the stakes in the issue or topic. Literature reviews are common examples of narrations in academic writing.

- Confirmation: The confirmation states all claims supporting the thesis and furnishes evidence for each claim, arranging this material in logical order—e.g. from most obvious to most subtle or strongest to weakest.

- Refutation and Concession: The refutation and concession discuss opposing views and anticipate reader objections without weakening the thesis, yet permitting as many oppositions as possible.

- Summation: The summation strengthens the argument while summarizing it, supplying a strong conclusion and showing readers the superiority of the author's solution.

Introduction

A classical argument's introduction must pique reader interest, get readers to perceive the author as a writer, and establish the author's position. Shocking statistics, new ways of restating issues, or quotations or anecdotes focusing the text can pique reader interest. Personal statements, parallel instances, or analogies can also begin introductions—so can bold thesis statements if the author believes readers will agree. Word choice is also important for establishing author image with readers. The introduction should typically narrow down to a clear, sound thesis statement. If readers cannot locate one sentence in the introduction explicitly stating the writer's position or the point they support, the writer probably has not refined the introduction sufficiently.

Narration and Confirmation

The narration part of a classical argument should create a context for the argument by explaining the issue to which the argument is responding, and by supplying any background information that influences the issue. Readers should understand the issues, alternatives, and stakes in the argument by the end of the narration to enable them to evaluate the author's claims equitably. The confirmation part of the classical argument enables the author to explain why they believe in the argument's thesis. The author builds a chain of reasoning by developing several individual supporting claims and explaining why that evidence supports each claim and also supports the overall thesis of the argument.

Refutation and Concession and Summation

The classical argument is the model for argumentative/persuasive writing, so authors often use it to establish, promote, and defend their positions. In the refutation aspect of the refutation and concession part of the argument, authors disarm reader opposition by anticipating and answering their possible objections, persuading them to accept the author's viewpoint. In the concession aspect, authors can concede those opposing viewpoints with which they agree. This can avoid weakening the author's thesis while establishing reader respect and goodwill for the author: all refutation and no concession can antagonize readers who disagree with the author's position. In the conclusion part of the classical argument, a less skilled writer might simply summarize or restate the thesis and related claims; however, this does not provide the argument with either momentum or closure. More skilled authors revisit the issues and the narration part of the argument, reminding readers of what is at stake.

Evaluating Reasoning and Evidence from Various Sources

Books as Resources
When a student has an assignment to research and write a paper, one of the first steps after determining the topic is to select research sources. The student may begin by conducting an Internet or library search of the topic, may refer to a reading list provided by the instructor, or may use an annotated bibliography of works related to the topic. To evaluate the worth of the book for the research paper, the student first considers the book title to get an idea of its content. Then the student can scan the book's table of contents for chapter titles and topics to get further ideas of their applicability to the topic. The student may also turn to the end of the book to look for an alphabetized index. Most academic textbooks and scholarly works have these; students can look up key topic terms to see how many are included and how many pages are devoted to them.

Journal Articles
Like books, journal articles are primary or secondary sources the student may need to use for researching any topic. To assess whether a journal article will be a useful source for a particular paper topic, a student can first get some idea about the content of the article by reading its title and subtitle, if any exists. Many journal articles, particularly scientific ones, include abstracts. These are brief summaries of the content. The student should read the abstract to get a more specific idea of whether the experiment, literature review, or other work documented is applicable to the paper topic. Students should also check the references at the end of the article, which today often contain links to related works for exploring the topic further.

Encyclopedias and Dictionaries
Dictionaries and encyclopedias are both reference books for looking up information alphabetically. Dictionaries are more exclusively focused on vocabulary words. They include each word's correct spelling, pronunciation, variants, part(s) of speech, definitions of one or more meanings, and examples used in a sentence. Some dictionaries provide illustrations of certain words when these inform the meaning. Some dictionaries also offer synonyms, antonyms, and related words under a word's entry. Encyclopedias, like dictionaries, often provide word pronunciations and definitions. However, they have broader scopes: one can look up entire subjects in encyclopedias, not just words, and find comprehensive, detailed information about historical events, famous people, countries, disciplines of study, and many other things. Dictionaries are for finding word meanings, pronunciations, and spellings; encyclopedias are for finding breadth and depth of information on a variety of topics.

Card Catalogs
A card catalog is a means of organizing, classifying, and locating the large numbers of books found in libraries. Without being able to look up books in library card catalogs, it would be virtually impossible to find them on library shelves. Card catalogs may be on traditional paper cards filed in drawers, or electronic catalogs accessible online; some libraries combine both. Books are shelved by subject area; subjects are coded using formal classification systems—standardized sets of rules for identifying and labeling books by subject and author. These assign each book a call number: a code indicating the classification system, subject, author, and title. Call numbers also function as bookshelf "addresses" where books can be located. Most public libraries use the Dewey Decimal Classification System. Most university, college, and research libraries use the Library of Congress Classification. Nursing students will also

encounter the National Institute of Health's National Library of Medicine Classification System, which major collections of health sciences publications utilize.

Databases

A database is a collection of digital information organized for easy access, updating, and management. Users can sort and search databases for information. One way of classifying databases is by content, i.e. full-text, numerical, bibliographical, or images. Another classification method used in computing is by organizational approach. The most common approach is a relational database, which is tabular and defines data so they can be accessed and reorganized in various ways. A distributed database can be reproduced or interspersed among different locations within a network. An object-oriented database is organized to be aligned with object classes and subclasses defining the data. Databases usually collect files like product inventories, catalogs, customer profiles, sales transactions, student bodies, and resources. An associated set of application programs is a database management system or database manager. It enables users to specify which reports to generate, control access to reading and writing data, and analyze database usage. Structured Query Language (SQL) is a standard computer language for updating, querying, and otherwise interfacing with databases.

Identifying Primary Sources in Various Media

A primary source is a piece of original work. This can include books, musical compositions, recordings, movies, works of visual art (paintings, drawings, photographs), jewelry, pottery, clothing, furniture, and other artifacts. Within books, primary sources may be of any genre. Whether nonfiction based on actual events or a fictional creation, the primary source relates the author's firsthand view of some specific event, phenomenon, character, place, process, ideas, field of study or discipline, or other subject matter. Whereas primary sources are original treatments of their subjects, secondary sources are a step removed from the original subjects; they analyze and interpret primary sources. These include journal articles, newspaper or magazine articles, works of literary criticism, political commentaries, and academic textbooks.

In the field of history, primary sources frequently include documents that were created around the same time period that they were describing, and most often produced by someone who had direct experience or knowledge of the subject matter. In contrast, secondary sources present the ideas and viewpoints of other authors about the primary sources; in history, for example, these can include books and other written works about the particular historical periods or eras in which the primary sources were produced. Primary sources pertinent in history include diaries, letters, statistics, government information, and original journal articles and books. In literature, a primary source might be a literary novel, a poem or book of poems, or a play. Secondary sources addressing primary sources may be criticism, dissertations, theses, and journal articles. Tertiary sources, typically reference works referring to primary and secondary sources, include encyclopedias, bibliographies, handbooks, abstracts, and periodical indexes.

In scientific fields, when scientists conduct laboratory experiments to answer specific research questions and test hypotheses, lab reports and reports of research results constitute examples of primary sources. When researchers produce statistics to support or refute hypotheses, those statistics are primary sources. When a scientist is studying some subject longitudinally or conducting a case study, they may keep a journal or diary. For example, Charles Darwin kept diaries of extensive notes on his studies during sea voyages on the *Beagle*, visits to the Galápagos Islands, etc.; Jean Piaget kept journals of observational notes for case studies of children's learning behaviors. Many scientists, particularly in past centuries, shared and discussed discoveries, questions, and ideas with colleagues through letters, which also constitute primary sources. When a scientist seeks to replicate another's experiment, the reported results, analysis, and commentary on the original work is a secondary source, as is a student's dissertation if it analyzes or discusses others' work rather than reporting original research or ideas.

ACT Writing Test

Elements of the Writing Process

Skilled writers undergo a series of steps that comprise the writing process. The purpose of adhering to a structured approach to writing is to develop clear, meaningful, coherent work.

The stages are pre-writing or planning, organizing, drafting/writing, revising, and editing. Not every writer will necessarily follow all five stages for every project, but will judiciously employ the crucial components of the stages for most formal or important work. For example, a brief informal response to a short reading passage may not necessitate the need for significant organization after idea generation, but larger assignments and essays will likely mandate use of the full process.

Pre-Writing/Planning
Brainstorming
One of the most important steps in writing is pre-writing. Before drafting an essay or other assignment, it's helpful to think about the topic for a moment or two, in order to gain a more solid understanding of what the task is. Then, spend about five minutes jotting down the immediate ideas that could work for the essay. **Brainstorming** is a way to get some words on the page and offer a reference for ideas when drafting. Scratch paper is provided for writers to use any pre-writing techniques such as webbing, freewriting, or listing. Some writers prefer using graphic organizers during this phase. The goal is to get ideas out of the mind and onto the page.

Freewriting
Like brainstorming, **freewriting** is another prewriting activity to help the writer generate ideas. This method involves setting a timer for two or three minutes and writing down all ideas that come to mind about the topic using complete sentences. Once time is up, writers should review the sentences to see what observations have been made and how these ideas might translate into a more unified direction for the topic. Even if sentences lack sense as a whole, freewriting is an excellent way to get ideas onto the page in the very beginning stages of writing. Using complete sentences can make this a bit more challenging than brainstorming, but overall it is a worthwhile exercise, as it may force the writer to come up with more complete thoughts about the topic.

Once the ideas are on the page, it's time for the writer to turn them into a solid plan for the essay. The best ideas from the brainstorming results can then be developed into a more formal outline.

Organizing
Although sometimes it is difficult to get going on the brainstorming or prewriting phase, once ideas start flowing, writers often find that they have amassed too many thoughts that will not make for a cohesive and unified essay. During the organization stage, writers should examine the generated ideas, hone in on the important ones central to their main idea, and arrange the points in a logical and effective manner. Writers may also determine that some of the ideas generated in the planning process need further elaboration, potentially necessitating the need for research to gather infortmation to fill the gaps.

Once a writer has chosen his or her thesis and main argument, selected the most applicable details and evidence, and eliminated the "clutter," it is time to strategically organize the ideas. This is often accomplished with an outline.

Outlining

An **outline** is a system used to organize writing. When composing essays, outlining is important because it helps writers organize important information in a logical pattern using Roman numerals. Usually, outlines start out with the main ideas and then branch out into subgroups or subsidiary thoughts or subjects. Not only do outlines provide a visual tool for writers to reflect on how events, ideas, evidence, or other key parts of the argument relate to one another, but they can also lead writers to a stronger conclusion. The sample below demonstrates what a general outline looks like:

I. Introduction
    1. Background
    2. Thesis statement
II. Body
    1. Point A
        a. Supporting evidence
        b. Supporting evidence
    2. Point B
        a. Supporting evidence
        b. Supporting evidence
    3. Point C
        a. Supporting evidence
        b. Supporting evidence
III. Conclusion
    1. Restate main points of the paper.
    2. End with something memorable.

Drafting/Writing

Now it comes time to actually write the essay. In this stage, writers should follow the outline they developed in the brainstorming process and try to incorporate the useful sentences penned in the freewriting exercise. The main goal of this phase is to put all the thoughts together in cohesive sentences and paragraphs.

It is helpful for writers to remember that their work here does not have to be perfect. This process is often referred to as **drafting** because writers are just creating a rough draft of their work. Because of this, writers should avoid getting bogged down on the small details.

Referencing Sources

Anytime a writer quotes or paraphrases another text, they will need to include a citation. A **citation** is a short description of the work that a quote or information came from. The style manual your teacher wants you to follow will dictate exactly how to format that citation. For example, this is how one would cite a book according to the APA manual of style:

- *Format:* Last name, First initial, Middle initial. (Year Published) *Book Title*. City, State: Publisher.
- *Example:* Sampson, M. R. (1989). *Diaries from an alien invasion*. Springfield, IL: Campbell Press.

Revising

Revising offers an opportunity for writers to polish things up. Putting one's self in the reader's shoes and focusing on what the essay actually says helps writers identify problems—it's a movement from the mindset of writer to the mindset of editor. The goal is to have a clean, clear copy of the essay.

The main goal of the revision phase is to improve the essay's flow, cohesiveness, readability, and focus. For example, an essay will make a less persuasive argument if the various pieces of evidence are scattered and presented illogically or clouded with unnecessary thought. Therefore, writers should consider their essay's structure and organization, ensuring that there are smooth transitions between sentences and paragraphs. There should be a discernable introduction and conclusion as well, as these crucial components of an essay provide readers with a blueprint to follow.

Additionally, if the writer includes copious details that do little to enhance the argument, they may actually distract readers from focusing on the main ideas and detract from the strength of their work. The ultimate goal is to retain the purpose or focus of the essay and provide a reader-friendly experience. Because of this, writers often need to delete parts of their essay to improve its flow and focus. Removing sentences, entire paragraphs, or large chunks of writing can be one of the toughest parts of the writing process because it is difficult to part with work one has done. However, ultimately, these types of cuts can significantly improve one's essay.

Lastly, writers should consider their voice and word choice. The voice should be consistent throughout and maintain a balance between an authoritative and warm style, to both inform and engage readers. One way to alter voice is through word choice. Writers should consider changing weak verbs to stronger ones and selecting more precise language in areas where wording is vague. In some cases, it is useful to modify sentence beginnings or to combine or split up sentences to provide a more varied sentence structure.

Editing
Rather than focusing on content (as is the aim in the revising stage), the **editing** phase is all about the mechanics of the essay: the syntax, word choice, and grammar. This can be considered the proofreading stage. Successful editing is what sets apart a messy essay from a polished document.

The following areas should be considered when proofreading:

- Sentence fragments
- Awkward sentence structure
- Run-on sentences
- Incorrect word choice
- Grammatical agreement errors
- Spelling errors
- Punctuation errors
- Capitalization errors

One of the most effective ways of identifying grammatical errors, awkward phrases, or unclear sentences is to read the essay out loud. Listening to one's own work can help move the writer from simply the author to the reader.

During the editing phase, it's also important to ensure the essay follows the correct formatting and citation rules as dictated by the assignment.

Recursive Writing Process
While the writing process may have specific steps, the good news is that the process is recursive, meaning the steps need not be completed in a particular order. Many writers find that they complete steps at the same time such as drafting and revising, where the writing and rearranging of ideas occur simultaneously or in very close order. Similarly, a writer may find that a particular section of a draft needs more development, and will go back to the prewriting stage to generate new ideas. The steps can be repeated

at any time, and the more these steps of the recursive writing process are employed, the better the final product will be.

Practice Makes Prepared Writers

Like any other useful skill, writing only improves with practice. While writing may come more easily to some than others, it is still a skill to be honed and improved. Regardless of a person's natural abilities, there is always room for growth in writing. Practicing the basic skills of writing can aid in preparations for the ACT.

One way to build vocabulary and enhance exposure to the written word is through reading. This can be through reading books, but reading of any materials such as newspapers, magazines, and even social media count towards practice with the written word. This also helps to enhance critical reading and thinking skills, through analysis of the ideas and concepts read. Think of each new reading experience as a chance to sharpen these skills.

Practice Test #1

English

Questions 1–15 are based on the following passage:

When Nathaniel Hawthorne wrote *The Scarlet Letter* in 1850, he became the first American author to contribute a mature tragic view of life (1) <u>in</u> the literature of the young United States. He developed a tragic vision that is fundamentally dark: man's inevitable moral downfall is determined by the workings of (2) <u>its own heart</u>. Yet Hawthorne's bleak vision also embraces the drama of the human heart, through which he depicts the heart as a redemptive agent, subtly affirming (3) <u>humanities</u> inherent goodness. He likens the human heart to a cavern. To a visitor, the mouth of the cavern is bright with sunlight and flowers, (4) <u>but a few feet in, the light dims and warmth turns to chill; the visitor stumbles, first in confusion, then in terror.</u> (5) <u>Further back</u>, a small gleam of light appears and the visitor hurries toward it, to find a scene much like that at the entrance of the cavern, only perfect. This, to Hawthorne, is the depth of (6) <u>human nature; the beauty that lies beyond fear and hopelessness.</u>

The novel relates the suffering of three people—Hester Prynne, Arthur Dimmesdale, and Roger Chillingworth—each possessing a proud heart that leads them to a choice between a natural morality (represented by the passion that derives from human love) (7) <u>and unnatural morality</u> (symbolized by the code of punishment the Puritan community adheres to). Studying the heart in the context of seventeenth-century Puritanism, Hawthorne focuses on the contradictions between the theological and intellectual definitions of sin, according to the Puritans, and the (8) <u>psychological affects</u> of applying them to the reality of their actions and lives. Within the (9) <u>rigid</u> moral setting of the New England Puritan community, he concentrates upon the sin of pride, fostered in the dim, shadowy hollows of the heart and soul. Man is inevitably faced with the destructive force of pride, and subsequently he is involved in the wrong and guilt it produces. He seeks salvation (the Calvinists believed (10) <u>it would be attained after an open confession of sin</u>), and although he recognizes the bond of sin he shares with all men, the penalty he must pay is one of (11) <u>individual, spiritual, psychological and even physical isolation</u>. (12) <u>The lives of Hawthorne's three protagonists can be described as a gradual awakening achieved through transition from deeds to emotions to comprehension of life's greater meaning</u>, a tri-part cadence (13) <u>that can neither be ignored nor avoided</u>. (14) <u>He shows how Hester's stalwart heart adjusts to the tragedy of her illicit love; how Arthur's heart, enfeebled by pride and lust, declines under sustained strain; and how Chillingworth's stagnant heart putrefies through the act of vengeance.</u> Life's tragedy, (15) <u>with the light and shadows that flit through it</u>, does not defeat Hester Prynne's magnificent heart, and this conclusion tempers Hawthorne's generally gloomy novel, lending a glint of light to his dark but not hopeless view of human nature.

1. The best replacement for the underlined portion would be:
    a. NO CHANGE
    b. to
    c. from
    d. with

2. The best replacement for the underlined portion would be:
    a. NO CHANGE
    b. her own heart
    c. his own heart
    d. people's own heart

3. The best replacement for the underlined portion would be:
    a. NO CHANGE
    b. humanities'
    c. humanitys
    d. humanity's

4. The best replacement for the underlined portion would be:
    a. NO CHANGE
    but a few feet in, the light dims and warmth turns to chill; the visitor stumbles first in confusion, then in terror.
    b. but a few feet in the light, dims and warmth turns to chill, the visitor stumbles, first in confusion, then in terror
    c. but a few feet in the light dims and warmth turns to chill, the visitor stumbles first in confusion then in terror
    d. but a few feet in the light dims and warmth turns to chill: the visitor stumbles first in confusion, then in terror

5. The best replacement for the underlined portion would be:
    a. NO CHANGE
    b. in the back
    c. to the back
    d. farther in

6. The best replacement for the underlined portion would be:
    a. NO CHANGE
    b. human nature. The beauty that lies beyond fear and hopelessness.
    c. human nature: the beauty that lies beyond fear and hopelessness.
    d. human nature (the beauty that lies beyond fear and hopelessness).

7. The best replacement for the underlined portion would be:
    a. NO CHANGE
    b. between a natural morality (represented by the passion that derives from human love) and an unnatural morality (symbolized by the code of punishment the Puritan community adheres to).
    c. between a natural morality represented by the passion that derives from human love and unnatural morality symbolized by the code of punishment the Puritan community adheres to.
    d. between a natural morality—represented by the passion that derives from human love—and unnatural morality, symbolized by the code of punishment the Puritan community adheres to.

8. The best replacement for the underlined portion would be:
    a. NO CHANGE
    b. psychological damage
    c. psychological changes
    d. psychological effects

9. Which choice most accurately conveys the meaning of the underlined word?
    a. Frightening
    b. Strict
    c. Harsh
    d. Dangerous

10. The best replacement for the underlined portion would be:
    a. NO CHANGE
    b. it would be awarded after an open confession of sin
    c. it would be purchased after an open confession of sin
    d. it would be appropriated after an open confession of sin

11. The best replacement for the underlined portion would be:
    a. NO CHANGE
    b. individual spiritual psychological and even physical isolation
    c. individual, spiritual, psychological, and even physical isolation
    d. individual spiritual, psychological, and even physical isolation

12. Which choice best simplifies the underlined statement?
    a. Through doing and feeling, Hawthorne's three protagonists comprehend the meaning of life
    b. When Hawthorne's three protagonists examine their deeds and the resulting emotions, each
    gradually comes to comprehend life's greater meaning
    c. Hawthorne's three protagonists gradually awaken during a transition from deeds to emotions to a
    comprehension of life's greater meaning
    d. Hawthorne's three protagonists each experience a gradual awakening as the emotions generated
    by
    their actions lead to an understanding of life's greater meaning

13. The best replacement for the underlined portion would be:
    a. NO CHANGE
    b. can either be ignored or avoided
    c. they should not ignore or avoid
    d. is inescapable

14. The paragraph needs a smooth transition from underlined sentence 13 to underlined underlined
sentence 14. Which choice would BEST accomplish this this?
    a. For one of the characters, the result is negative, and for two it is positive.
    b. The process of awakening is difficult for all three characters.
    c. Hawthorne intimately analyzes his characters, exposing the spontaneous movements of their hearts.
    d. This is where Hawthorne's tragic vision becomes clear.

15. Where would the underlined portion fit best in the sentence?
   a. NO CHANGE
   b. After *Hester's magnificent heart*
   c. After *and this conclusion*
   d. After *generally gloomy novel*

Questions 16 – 30 are based on the following passage:

The vast (16) <u>industrialization of Europe which took place between 1760 and 1840 was perhaps the most significant watershed</u> period in the history of Europe. It was a time of astronomical growth and progress for Europeans as a whole, yet it was simultaneously a wretched and dehumanizing period for the majority of European individuals. Many problems—economic, social, and political—were either created or magnified by the Industrial Revolution: (17) <u>problems which threatened European society</u> not with annihilation but with massive change in the form of a social revolution that would shift the distribution of political might and change class structure.

The Industrial Revolution touched and altered almost every aspect of the economic and political life of Europe prior to 1760, which, in turn, (18) <u>changed</u> the existing social order. (19) <u>With roots digging deeply into the past as the thirteenth century</u>, when capitalism and commerce began to develop, industrialization slowly became (20) <u>inevitable</u>. It was aided by a gradual expansion of the market, a demand for more goods by an increasing number of consumers, and the step-by-step freedom of private enterprise from government control. (21) <u>Industrialization began in earnest in the textile industry of Great Britain, and, due to progress in the field of technological innovations, caused a huge upswing in the amount of money necessary to establish a factory. Industry became the new source of wealth, (22) which had formerly been land, but the power remained concentrated within a small group of rich men—the capitalists.</u> The existence of this wealthy class directly contrasted with that of the impoverished working class (people who had once worked the land, until they were forced by industrialization to undertake factory labor in order to survive). The juxtaposition of a small (23) <u>number</u> of people, who held great wealth, with a population for whom extreme and widespread poverty was inescapable, was one of the greatest problems the Industrial Revolution created.

The plight of the industrial family was a shameful aspect of the modernization of Europe. Forced to migrate to areas rich in coal, (24) <u>where filthy, violence-ridden cities have sprung up</u>, the people of agrarian communities encountered suffering, despondency, and poverty. (25) <u>Wages were perpetually too low, and employment was always uncertain</u>. Housing was damp, dirty, cramped, and poorly ventilated, leading to sickness and the spread of disease. Death by starvation was not uncommon, as food was scarce and often unfit to eat.

Child labor was another ugly product of the Industrial Revolution. To help supply their families with the bare minimum of food, clothing, and shelter, children as young as five years old were (26) <u>obliged</u> to (27) <u>work thirteen hours a day in factories six days a week</u>. (28) <u>Half starved; unable to find respite from extreme heat and cold; beaten, kicked, and bruised by overseers, these children</u> were blighted by excessive misery.

<u>The problems created or aggravated by the Industrial Revolution—unfair distribution of wealth, squalid living conditions for much of the working class, child labor, and lack of education—forced a moral adaptation on the part of Europeans. (29) And from the new mindset, the middle class emerged.</u>

16. The best replacement for the underlined portion would be:

   a. NO CHANGE

   b. industrialization of Europe, which took place between 1760 and 1840 was perhaps the most significant watershed

   c. industrialization of Europe, which took place between 1760 and 1840, was perhaps the most significant watershed

   d. industrialization of Europe which took place, between 1760 and 1840, was perhaps the most significant watershed

17. The best replacement for the underlined portion would be:

   a. NO CHANGE

   b. problems threatened European society

   c. problems threatening to European society

   d. problems that threatened European society

18. In the context of the essay as a whole, which of the following words is the most accurate substitution for the underlined portion?

   a. transfigured

   b. disrupted

   c. destroyed

   d. transformed

19. The best replacement for the underlined portion would be:

   a. NO CHANGE

   b. With roots, digging deeply into the past as the thirteenth century

   c. With roots digging as deeply into the past as the thirteenth century

   d. With roots that were digging deeply into the past as the thirteenth century

20. Is the underlined word the most appropriate word choice?

   a. Yes, "inevitable" is most appropriate.

   b. No, "indelible" is more appropriate.

   c. No, "inadvertent" is more appropriate.

   d. No, "inadvisable" is more appropriate.

21. A transition sentence is needed to improve the flow from the sentence with number 21 to the following sentence. Which of the following sentences best accomplishes the transition?

   a. The demand for large amounts of capital was met by a small group of wealthy investors.

   b. Therefore, the need of large capitalists was predominant.

   c. Capitalists, with their deep pockets, came to the rescue.

   d. The economic theory of supply and demand was born.

22. The underlined sentence is awkward. Which choice below is the clearest rewrite?

   a. Land, formerly the source of wealth, was overshadowed by industry, dominated by rich capitalists.

   b. Capitalists invested in industry, which replaced land as the primary source of wealth. As a result, power was concentrated in the hands of the capitalists.

   c. By investing their capital in industry, the capitalists changed the source of wealth from land to industry and retained most of the power.

   d. Formerly the major source of wealth, land was replaced by industry, and the capitalists held all the power.

23. The best replacement for the underlined portion would be:
    a. NO CHANGE
    b. amount
    c. group
    d. class

24. The best replacement for the underlined portion would be:
    a. NO CHANGE
    b. where filthy, violence-ridden, cities have sprung up
    c. where filthy, violence-ridden cities had sprung up
    d. where filthy, violence ridden cities have sprung up

25. The best replacement for the underlined portion would be:
    a. NO CHANGE
    b. Wages were perpetually too low; and employment was always uncertain.
    c. Wages were perpetually too low, and, employment was always uncertain.
    d. Wages were perpetually too low and employment was always uncertain.

26. The best replacement for the underlined portion would be:
    a. NO CHANGE
    b. impounded
    c. apprenticed
    d. conscripted

27. The best replacement for the underlined portion would be:
    a. work thirteen hours a day, in factories, six days a week
    b. work thirteen hours a day in factories six days a week
    c. work thirteen hours a day in factories, with only Sundays off
    d. work in factories for thirteen hours a day, six days a week

28. The punctuation in the underlined portion is technically correct but awkward. Which of the following is the clearest rewrite with correct punctuation?
    a. Half starved, unable to find respite from extreme heat and cold, beaten, kicked, and bruised by overseers, these children were blighted
    b. Half starved, unable to find respite from extreme heat and cold, and, beaten, kicked, and bruised by overseers, these children were blighted
    c. These half-starved children, unable to find respite from extreme heat and cold, were beaten, kicked, and bruised by overseers and blighted
    d. Half starved, these children who were unable to find respite from extreme heat and cold were beaten, kicked, and bruised by overseers, and they were blighted

29. Is there a weakness in this conclusion?
    a. No, it is fine as is.
    b. It does not mention capitalists.
    c. It contains erroneous information.
    d. It contains extraneous information.

30. Is there an outstanding flaw in the essay as a whole?
    a. No, it is fine as is.
    b. The prose is too dramatic.
    c. It does not cover political change.
    d. It is unfair to the capitalists.

Questions 31–45 are based on the following passage:

The escalating rate of obesity in the United States is a major health issue facing all healthcare providers and (31) <u>faculties</u>. Today, at Carter Cullen Medical Center, a community hospital in (32) <u>Wayland, Massachusetts</u>, a simple perioperative step—highlighting body mass index (BMI, determined by dividing weight by height) on surgery schedules and preoperative checklists—is saving lives. In 2014, events involving two patients with high (33) <u>BMI's</u> triggered eighteen months of focused teamwork and communication that resulted in the establishment of a groundbreaking early notification protocol. As a consequence, the healthcare professionals at Carter Cullen Medical Center are better equipped to care for patients who are morbidly obese.

Obesity carries many risks, one of which is sleep apnea. (34) <u>Sleep apnea, in turn, causes problems with intubation during surgery and disrupts the administration of anesthetics</u> or oxygen. Additional adipose tissue in the neck area prevents patients from hyperextending their necks properly. During intubation, the anesthesiologist cannot visualize the vocal cords (35) <u>if the patients neck</u> is not hyperextended, and a fiber-optic intubation device must be inserted. But such a device was not regularly available in Carter Cullen's operating rooms; (36) <u>the equipment was stocked only if difficulty was expected</u>. In the first event, an obese patient needed to be intubated, there was unanticipated difficulty with the intubation, and the patient died.

Another life-threatening risk of obesity is rhabdomyolysis. In the second event, an obese patient recovering from prolonged total joint replacement surgery was resting in one position for an (37) <u>unreasonable</u> amount of time. The patient's weight caused muscle fibers (38) <u>to break down, and release a pigment—harmful to the kidneys—</u>into (39) <u>their</u> circulation. Renal failure and death followed.

These two deaths spurred Carter Cullen Medical Center to develop a program to (40) <u>insure</u> that obese patients are safe in the operating room and in post-op recovery. An extensive task force was formed to explore why the deaths occurred and determine preventive precautions.

The result was a BMI awareness tracking procedure that begins with surgery schedulers in doctors' offices, who now include (41) <u>weight and age</u> information for all patients when scheduling a procedure. If a patient's BMI is thirty-five or higher, it is prominently highlighted on the surgery schedule, so that staff know to prepare the operating room (42) <u>accordingly</u>. (43) <u>All operating room beds are now equipped with pressure-relief mattresses, to distribute a patient's body mass over a broader surface area.</u> The nursing quality council received specialized training in caring for high-BMI patients, and new hires take a mandatory electronic learning program that emphasizes recording BMI on confidential surgery schedules. In addition, the task force established a BMI sensitivity and understanding training program.

<u>These measures have been a success. Since 2016, when the quality care project was fully implemented, of one hundred charts tracked, ninety-one percent included the BMI on the surgery schedule, and ninety-six percent included it on the preoperative checklist.</u>

31. Which, if any, of the following choices is the most accurate choice to replace the underlined word?
    a. NO CHANGE
    b. facilities
    c. cardiologists
    d. the American Obesity Association

32. Which, if any, of the following choices is the most accurate choice to replace the underlined words?
    a. NO CHANGE
    b. Wayland Massachusetts
    c. Wayland, Massachusets
    d. a small Massachusetts town

33. Which, if any, of the following choices is the most accurate choice to replace the underlined word?
    a. NO CHANGE
    b. BMIs
    c. body mass indexes
    d. body mass indices

34. Which, if any, of the following choices is the most accurate choice to replace the underlined words?
    a. NO CHANGE
    b. Sleep apnea, in turn, caused problems with intubation during surgery and disrupted the administration of anesthetics
    c. Sleep apnea, in turn, can cause problems with intubation during surgery that disrupt the administration of anesthetics
    d. Sleep apnea, in turn, causes problems with intubation and the administration of anesthetics

35. Which, if any, of the following choices is the most accurate choice to replace the underlined words?
    a. NO CHANGE
    b. if the patient neck
    c. if the patient's neck
    d. if the patients' neck

36. Which, if any, of the following choices is the most accurate choice to replace the underlined words?
    a. NO CHANGE
    b. the equipment was stocked if difficulty only was expected
    c. the equipment only was stocked if difficulty was expected
    d. only the equipment was stocked if difficulty was expected

37. Within the context of this paragraph, which word makes the most sense?
    a. NO CHANGE
    b. outrageous
    c. unacceptable
    d. extended

38. Which choice clarifies the underlined passage and is grammatically correct?
    a. to break down, and release a pigment harmful to the kidneys
    b. to break down, and release a pigment—harmful to the kidneys
    c. to break down and release a pigment harmful to the kidneys
    d. to break down—and release a pigment—harmful to the kidneys—

39. Which of the following words is a grammatically correct replacement for the underlined portion?
    a. NO CHANGE
    b. They're
    c. There
    d. Its

40. Which, if any, of the following choices is the most accurate choice to replace the underlined word?
    a. NO CHANGE
    b. ensure
    c. assure
    d. invalidate

41. Which, if any, of the following choices is the most accurate choice to replace the underlined word?
    a. NO CHANGE
    b. weight and gender
    c. weight and height
    d. weight and race

42. What preparation needs to be made for the operating rooms to be prepared "accordingly"?
    a. All the instruments must be thoroughly sterilized.
    b. A fiber-optic intubation device must be on hand.
    c. The operating table must be equipped with a scale.
    d. A back-up anesthesiologist must be in attendance.

43. How do the mattresses mentioned in the underlined sentence help patients?
    a. They make the patients more comfortable than regular mattresses.
    b. They are soft, which helps muscles relax.
    c. They distribute body weight more evenly than regular mattresses, so pressure is minimized.
    d. They massage the body, which makes sleeping easier.

44. Which sentence would make the most logical conclusion to the essay?
    a. No intubation emergencies or positioning incidents have occurred in patients with a high BMI since January 1, 2016.
    b. Doctors, nurses, and administrative staff credit the task force for this huge success.
    c. A cost-benefit task force has been convened to assess the financial impact of the new program.
    d. Carter Cullen Medical Center hopes to share the new program with other hospitals across the country.

45. The writer has been asked to provide a subtitle for this essay. Which choice best summarizes the content?
    a. New Early Notification Protocol at Carter Cullen Medical Center
    b. Hospital Task Force Saves Lives
    c. Local Hospital Has Success with Obese Patients
    d. How One Hospital Prevents Perioperative Complications in Obese Patient

Questions 46–60 are based on the following passage:

(Paragraph Number 1) Cerebrovascular accident, commonly known as stroke, is the fifth leading cause of death in the United States, and it (46) <u>affects</u> approximately 795,000 Americans each year. (47) <u>The risk of stroke varies by demographics and lifestyle factors such as age (fifty years or older), gender (female), race (African American, American Indian, and Alaskan native), geography (southeastern states), disease, and lifestyle components (including, but not limited to: exercise, eating habits, use of alcohol and/or illicit drugs, cigarette smoking, stress, quality of life, and perceived happiness)</u>.

(48) <u>(Paragraph Number 2)</u> What exactly is a stroke? It is a sudden interruption in cerebral (brain) function that (49) <u>lasts more than twenty-four hours. Stroke can result in death, and is caused by an acute disruption of blood flow coupled with insufficient oxygen reaching the brain</u>. A stroke can be large and catastrophic, ending in death; mild, with the person who had the stroke eventually recovering most normal functions; or anywhere between these two (50) <u>extremes</u>.

(Paragraph Number 3) The two main types of stroke are ischemic and hemorrhagic. Ischemic stroke occurs when a blood clot blocks an artery in the central nervous system (CNS). (51) <u>The blockage disrupts the flow of oxygen-rich blood to CNS tissue and to the brain to the extent that the supply of oxygen and glucose is insufficient to support ongoing metabolism.</u> Thrombotic stroke and embolic stroke are two subtypes of ischemic stroke. In thrombotic stroke, a blood clot or atherosclerotic plaque develops (52) <u>locally</u> to create blockage. (53) <u>In embolic stroke, a blood clot or atherosclerotic plaque develops elsewhere, such as in the heart, breaks apart, and travels in the bloodstream without</u>

<u>blocking blood flow until it reaches a central nervous system artery, then it travels through the artery up to the brain, lodging there.</u>

(Paragraph Number 4) (54) <u>Headache, nausea, vomiting, numbness, and loss of consciousness are</u>

<u>all warning signs of a possible stroke these symptoms require immediate medical attention to prevent</u>

<u>damage to—or complete loss of—brain cells. The three most common symptoms of stroke are varying degrees of facial drooping, unilateral limb weakness, and speech difficulty. Noncontrast computed tomography (CT) scans can detect mass lesions, such as a tumor or an abscess, and an acute hemorrhage. Strokes can also cause depression and a loss of the ability to control emotions. (55)</u>

(Paragraph Number 5) Hemorrhagic stroke is caused when a blood vessel ruptures, sending blood into the surrounding brain tissue. Intracerebral hemorrhage is one subtype of hemorrhagic stroke and is characterized by bleeding within brain tissue. Subarachnoid hemorrhage is a second subtype and occurs when bleeding is within the space between the arachnoid and pia mater membranes of the meninges, the connective tissue around the brain. Bleeding within the brain is a serious condition, (56) <u>as the blood leaked</u> can destroy brain tissue and impairment can happen within a matter of minutes.

(Paragraph Number 6) With both ischemic stroke and hemorrhagic stroke, structural damage in the central nervous system can disrupt connecting pathways, leading to significant loss of neurologic function and disability. (57) <u>The development of neurological disease may be a consequence of stroke-associated disruption of certain neuronal pathways.</u>

46. Which choice, if any, would be an acceptable substitute for the underlined portion?
    a. destroys
    b. effects
    c. kills
    d. afflicts

47. Carlos is a 27-year-old Hispanic male who lives in New York, and he maintains a healthy lifestyle by eating wholesome foods, exercising regularly, and getting an average of eight hours of sleep per night. He enjoys an occasional beer or glass of wine on weekends, but he does not drink to excess and has never used illicit drugs. He does not smoke, he practices yoga and meditation to control stress, and he is generally satisfied with where he is in his life today. According to the underlined passage, Carlos:
    a. will never have a stroke if he continues living as he does now
    b. will never have a stroke because he is not a "match" in any of the categories
    c. will have a stroke if he stops exercising, gains weight, and starts smoking cigarettes
    d. might be one of the Americans who has a stroke

48. If this sentence were added at the end of Paragraph Number 2, what would the effect be? "The prevalence of pseudobulbar affect among stroke survivors is estimated to be between eleven and fifty-two percent."
    a. It would be confusing because the information is irrelevant to the essay.
    b. It would be helpful because it adds information that supports the topic of the paragraph.
    c. It would be confusing because pseudobulbar affect has not been introduced previously.
    d. It would be helpful because it cites a relatively positive stroke survival statistic.

49. What is the most logical ordering of the three items in the underlined passage?
    a. NO CHANGE
    b. is caused by an acute disruption of blood flow, lasts more than twenty-four hours, and can result in death
    c. can result in death, lasts more than twenty-four hours, and is caused by an acute disruption of blood flow
    d. can result in death, is caused by an acute disruption of blood flow, lasts more than twenty-four hours

50. In the context of the sentence, which word is the closest synonym to the underlined word?
    a. Spectrums
    b. States
    c. Poles
    d. Positions

51. Where is the best place to insert a comma in the underlined passage?
    a. The punctuation is correct as is.
    b. The blockage disrupts the flow of oxygen-rich blood to CNS tissue and to the brain, to the extent that the supply of oxygen and glucose is insufficient to support ongoing metabolism.
    c. The blockage disrupts the flow of oxygen-rich blood to CNS tissue, and to the brain to the extent that the supply of oxygen and glucose is insufficient to support ongoing metabolism.
    d. The blockage disrupts the flow of oxygen-rich blood, to CNS tissue and to the brain to the extent that the supply of oxygen and glucose is insufficient to support ongoing metabolism.

52. In the context of this paragraph, what does the word "locally" word mean?
    a. In the brain
    b. In the CNS
    c. Anywhere in the arteries where there are clots and plaque
    d. In the fat cells

53. There is a semicolon missing from this run-on sentence. What is the correct position for it?
    a. In embolic stroke, a blood clot or atherosclerotic plaque develops elsewhere, such as in the heart; breaks apart, and travels in the bloodstream without blocking blood flow until it reaches a central nervous system artery, then it travels through the artery up to the brain, lodging there.
    b. In embolic stroke, a blood clot or atherosclerotic plaque develops elsewhere, such as in the heart, breaks apart, and travels in the bloodstream without blocking blood flow until it reaches a central nervous system artery; then it travels through the artery up to the brain, lodging there.
    c. In embolic stroke, a blood clot or atherosclerotic plaque develops elsewhere; such as in the heart, breaks apart, and travels in the bloodstream without blocking blood flow until it reaches a central nervous system artery, then it travels through the artery up to the brain, lodging there.
    d. In embolic stroke, a blood clot or atherosclerotic plaque develops elsewhere, such as in the heart, breaks apart; and travels in the bloodstream without blocking blood flow until it reaches a central nervous system artery, then it travels through the artery up to the brain, lodging there.

54. Which punctuation mark is the correct one to place between "stroke" and "these"?
    a. Slash (/)
    b. Dash (—)
    c. Semicolon (;)
    d. Period (.)

55. Which sentence, if any, interrupts the flow of the discussion in the paragraph?
    a. None.
    b. The sentence beginning "The three most common symptoms..."
    c. The sentence beginning "Noncontrast computed tomography..."
    d. The sentence beginning "Strokes can also cause depression..."

56. Which is correct?
    a. NO CHANGE
    b. as the blood is leaked can destroy brain tissue
    c. as the blood is leaked, can destroy brain tissue
    d. because as blood leaked, it can destroy brain tissue

57. Which outline of types and subtypes of stroke is correct?

I. Ischemic
    A. Thrombotic
    B. **Atherosclerotic**
II. Hemorrhagic
    A. Intracerebral
    B. Subarachnoid

I. Ischemic
    A. Thrombotic
    B. Embolic
II. Hemorrhagic
    A. Intracerebral
    B. Subarachnoid

I. Hemorrhagic
    A. Thrombotic
    B. Embolic
II. Ischemic
    A. Intracerebral
    B. Subarachnoid

I. Ischemic
    A. Thrombotic
    B. Embolic
II. Hemorrhagic
    A. Arachnoid
    B. Pia mater

58. the paragraphs in the essay are numbered 1-6. Which ordering structure is most logical?
    a. 1, 2, 3, 5, 6, 4
    b. 1, 2, 3, 4, 6, 5
    c. 1, 2, 4, 3, 5, 6
    d. 1, 4, 2, 3, 5, 6

59. Working with the paragraphs as numbered, in which paragraph would the following information most logically be located? "The pathophysiology of hemorrhagic stroke is primarily attributed to the presence of blood in extracellular tissues of the central nervous system. The primary damage to surrounding brain tissue is related to the mass effect of excess blood on neural structures."
    a. Paragraph number 2
    b. Paragraph number 3
    c. Paragraph number 5
    d. Paragraph number 6

60. Which of the following statements is false?

    a. Approximately 795,000 Americans die of stroke each year.

    b. Thrombotic stroke and embolic stroke are subtypes of ischemic stroke, and they are caused by blood clots.

    c. The primary damage to brain tissue is related to the mass effect of excess blood.

    d. Both types of stroke disrupt the normal activity of structures in the CNS.

Questions 61–75 are based on the following passage:

The concept of three-ness, (61) <u>embodied</u> by triplets, triads, and trios, is crucial to Indo-European societies as a way of creating order and stability within the social structure. (62) <u>The significance of the notion of three-ness is manifested in the literature of these cultures, which abounds with numerous events, occurring in patterns of three, that radically affect the lives of the main characters </u>and (63) <u>those of there families, friends, and foes.</u> In no body of literature, perhaps, is this more (64) <u>distinctly and consistently</u> seen than in that of the early Icelandic (65) <u>inhabitants</u>. (66) <u>The sagas produced by the Icelanders are surfeited with images of three, minor and major; it is in the later, and most widely acclaimed sagas (</u>*The Saga of Gisli, Laxdaela Saga,* and *Njal's Saga*)<u>, that three-ness is applied most skillfully.</u>

Saga authors exercised authorial control by using three-ness to create a balanced, rhythmic, organically unified fiction grounded in historical fact. (67) <u>There are two levels of significance in how they applied the concept of three. </u>The first level consists of instances in which the author mentions the number three (or multiples of three) that are minor in import. For example, three is widely used to name the number of sons the saga-man has, or the number of days he spends visiting a friend. Small multiples of three, such as fifteen and eighteen, mark the number of warriors fighting on either side in a skirmish, while greater multiples, such as sixty, 120, and three hundred are predominately associated with wealth or livestock. (68) <u>These recurring instances of three-ness serve a dual purpose. (69) Not only do they create a regular, periodic cadence—a steady underlying tempo—that links all of the sections of the saga together, but they also provide, by means of the (70) tripod-like sense of proportion, an equilibrium associated with the number three: a satisfying feeling of balance.</u>

(71) <u>The third level of relevance concerning the authorial application of three-ness deals with the aesthetic structure of the sagas.</u> It consists of the division of each saga into three sections, plot incidents yoked together in clusters of three, the reenactment of a specific deed or action three times, and the combination of several types of the minor instances of three-ness within the body of one episode that is particularly important in the life of the saga-man. (72) <u>For instance in Part III, Chapter III of the saga, the saga-man might slay an archenemy a third of the way through the third night of his residence at his adversary's abode, three villages away from his own.</u>

The application of imagination to the quantitative and qualitative use of the notion of three-ness did not suddenly appear, fully established and perfected, in the earliest of Icelandic literature. <u>Rather, it was gradually introduced, adapted, modified, and improved upon by many authors until it reached an artistically sophisticated stage. The frequency and significance of the usage of the number three increases in richness as the sagas progress chronologically according to their dates of composition.</u>

61. The definition of the underlined word is "to show in concrete form," and it is not entirely appropriate in this context. Which choice is most accurate?
    a. Marked
    b. Earmarked
    c. Included
    d. Represented

62. Which word or phrase should be eliminated to make the sentence less wordy?
    a. The significance of
    b. the notion of
    c. of these cultures
    d. numerous

63. If there is an error in the underlined sentence, what is the error?
    a. NO ERROR
    b. "Abounds" should be "abound."
    c. "There" should be "their."
    d. There should not be a comma before "and foes."

64. Choose the pair of words that is the closest substitute for "distinctly and consistently."
    a. Discerningly and constantly
    b. Clearly and uniformly
    c. Definitely and evenly
    d. Easily and transparently

65. What is the closest synonym to the underlined word?
    a. Dwellers
    b. Authors
    c. Cultures
    d. Persons

66. This sentence originally appeared at the end of the first paragraph, but it was later deleted: "The sagas are so noticeably saturated with trinities, threesomes, and treble happenings that the modern reader almost comes away from reading them with the numeral three indelibly stamped on her consciousness." What is the best reason for its deletion?
    a. It says the modern reader is female, which excludes the ones who are male.
    b. "Trinities, threesomes, and treble happenings" echoes the first sentence's "triplets, triads, and trios" and seems a bit forced, especially "treble happenings."
    c. What happens to the modern reader is irrelevant.
    d. The writer cannot possibly know the impact the repetition of threes has on anyone but his or her own self.

67. Which sentence would be the clearest, if inserted in this paragraph?
    a. There are two levels of significance to how they applied the concept of three.
    b. How they applied the concept of three has two levels.
    c. They applied the concept of three on two significant levels.
    d. There are two levels of significance to the application of three.

68. The underlined passage begins a new topic. This passage and the rest of the paragraph would work best as a separate paragraph. Where should the new paragraph be located?
    a. Immediately after the paragraph it is currently in
    b. Immediately after the first paragraph
    c. Immediately before the last paragraph
    d. Immediately after the last paragraph

69. Which is the clearest way of breaking this sentence into two sentences?
    a. They create a regular, periodic cadence—a steady underlying tempo—that links all of the sections of the saga together. They also provide, by means of the tripod-like sense of proportion, an equilibrium associated with the number three: a satisfying feeling of balance.
    b. Not only do they create a regular, periodic cadence that links all of the sections of the saga together. They also provide, by means of the tripod-like sense of proportion, an equilibrium associated with the number three.
    c. Not only do they create a regular, periodic cadence—a steady underlying tempo—that links all of the sections of the saga together. But they also provide, by means of the tripod-like sense of proportion, an equilibrium associated with the number three: a satisfying feeling of balance.
    d. A regular, periodic cadence—a steady underlying tempo—that links all of the sections of the saga together is created. Also, an equilibrium associated with the number three, a satisfying feeling of balance, is provided by means of the tripod-like sense of proportion.

70. What other image might the writer use to describe the "tripod-like" sense of proportion?
    a. A drawing compass
    b. A tricycle
    c. A three-legged dog
    d. A three-legged stool

71. Where is the error in the underlined passage?
    a. The word "aesthetic" doesn't make sense in this context.
    b. The word "chiefly" should be inserted after "deals."
    c. There are only two levels of relevance.
    d. Saga-men, not authors, apply the concept of three-ness.

72. In this sentence, one comma is missing. Where should it be inserted?
    a. After "instance"
    b. After "residence"
    c. After "Chapter III"
    d. After "archenemy"

73. Why was three-ness so important to the early Icelanders?
    a. They found it easiest to count and group things, such as livestock, by threes.
    b. Three was a significant number in their religion.
    c. It was a way to impose order.
    d. They needed a way to make their literature unique.

74. What is the major flaw in this essay?
    a. There's no mathematical back-up to show why three is so important.
    b. It doesn't explain how order and stability are created through the use of multiple threes.
    c. The concluding paragraph is off-topic.
    d. The examples are too complicated to follow easily.

75. Which idea is not supported in the essay?

a. The concept of three lends a sense of unity and proportion to the sagas.

b. Saga authors demonstrate awareness of the need of an aesthetic element by representing three-ness in the structure of their sagas.

c. Saga authors were interested in both telling a good story and the mechanics of writing.

d. The logical symmetry of the numbers two and four is equal to the balance of three.

Reading

Passage I: Literature

The following passage is taken from Chapter 6 of Sense and Sensibility, *by Jane Austen:*

The first part of their journey was performed in too melancholy a disposition to be otherwise than tedious and unpleasant. But as they drew toward the end of it, their interest in the appearance of a country which they were to inhabit overcame their dejection, and a view of Barton Valley as they entered it gave them cheerfulness. It was a pleasant fertile spot, well wooded, and rich in pasture. After winding along it for more than a mile, they reached their own house. A small green court was the whole of its demesne in front; and a neat wicket gate admitted them into it.

As a house, Barton Cottage, though small, was comfortable and compact; but as a cottage it was defective, for the building was regular, the roof was tiled, the window shutters were not painted green, nor were the walls covered with honeysuckles. A narrow passage led directly through the house into the garden behind. On each side of the entrance was a sitting room, about sixteen feet square; and beyond them were the offices and the stairs. Four bed-rooms and two garrets formed the rest of the house. It had not been built many years and was in good repair. In comparison of Norland, it was poor and small indeed!—but the tears which recollection called forth as they entered the house were soon dried away. They were cheered by the joy of the servants on their arrival, and each for the sake of the others resolved to appear happy. It was very early in September; the season was fine, and from first seeing the place under the advantage of good weather, they received an impression in its favour which was of material service in recommending it to their lasting approbation.

The situation of the house was good. High hills rose immediately behind, and at no great distance on each side; some of which were open downs, the others cultivated and woody. The village of Barton was chiefly on one of these hills, and formed a pleasant view from the cottage windows. The prospect in front was more extensive; it commanded the whole of the valley, and reached into the country beyond. The hills which surrounded the cottage terminated the valley in that direction; under another name, and in another course, it branched out again between two of the steepest of them.

With the size and furniture of the house Mrs. Dashwood was upon the whole well satisfied; for though her former style of life rendered many additions to the latter indispensable, yet to add and improve was a delight to her; and she had at this time ready money enough to supply all that was wanted of greater elegance to the apartments. "As for the house itself, to be sure," said she, "it is too small for our family, but we will make ourselves tolerably comfortable for the present, as it is too late in the year for improvements. Perhaps in the spring, if I have plenty of money, as I dare say I shall, we may think about building. These parlors are both too small for such parties of our friends as I hope to see often collected here; and I have some thoughts of throwing the passage into one of them with perhaps a part of the other, and so leave the remainder of that other for an entrance; this, with a new drawing room which may be easily added, and a bed-chamber and garret above, will make it a very snug little cottage. I could wish the stairs were handsome. But one must not expect every thing; though I suppose it would be no difficult matter to widen them. I shall see how much I am before-hand with the world in the spring, and we will plan our improvements accordingly."

In the mean time, till all these alterations could be made from the savings of an income of five hundred a-year by a woman who never saved in her life, they were wise enough to be contented with the house as it was; and each of them was busy in arranging their particular concerns, and endeavoring, by placing around them books and other possessions, to form themselves a home. Marianne's pianoforte was unpacked and properly disposed of; and Elinor's drawings were affixed to the walls of their sitting room.

In such employments as these they were interrupted soon after breakfast the next day by the entrance of their landlord, who called to welcome them to Barton, and to offer them every accommodation from his own house and garden in which theirs might at present be deficient. Sir John Middleton was a good looking man about forty. He had formerly visited at Stanhill, but it was too long for his young cousins to remember him. His countenance was thoroughly good-humoured; and his manners were as friendly as the style of his letter. Their arrival seemed to afford him real satisfaction, and their comfort to be an object of real solicitude to him. He said much of his earnest desire of their living in the most sociable terms with his family, and pressed them so cordially to dine at Barton Park every day till they were better settled at home, that, though his entreaties were carried to a point of perseverance beyond civility, they could not give offence. His kindness was not confined to words; for within an hour after he left them, a large basket full of garden stuff and fruit arrived from the park, which was followed before the end of the day by a present of game.

1. What is the point of view in this passage?
   a. Third-person omniscient
   b. Second-person
   c. First-person
   d. Third-person objective

2. Which of the following events occurred first?
   a. Sir John Middleton stopped by for a visit.
   b. The servants joyfully cheered for the family.
   c. Mrs. Dashwood discussed improvements to the cottage.
   d. Elinor hung her drawings up in the sitting room.

3. Over the course of the passage, the Dashwoods' attitude shifts. Which statement best describes that shift?
   a. From appreciation of the family's former life of privilege to disdain for the family's new landlord
   b. From confidence in the power of the family's wealth to doubt in the family's ability to survive
   c. From melancholy about leaving Norland to excitement about reaching Barton Cottage in the English countryside
   d. From cheerfulness about the family's expedition to anxiety about the upkeep of such a big home

4. Which of the following is a theme of this passage?
    a. All-conquering love
    b. Power of wealth
    c. Wisdom of experience
    d. Reality vs. expectations

5. At the start of paragraph five, the narrator says, "till all these alterations could be made from the savings of an income of five hundred a-year by a woman who never saved in her life, they were wise enough to be contented with the house as it was." What does the narrator mean?
    a. The family is going through a transition phase.
    b. Mrs. Dashwood needs to obtain meaningful employment.
    c. The family is going through a growth phase.
    d. The Dashwood children need to be concerned about the future.

6. What is the relationship between the new landlord and the Dashwoods?
    a. He is a former social acquaintance.
    b. He is one of their cousins.
    c. He is Mrs. Dashwood's father.
    d. He is a long-time friend of the family.

7. Why does the narrator describe the generosity of Sir John Middleton?
    a. To identify one of many positive traits that a landlord should possess.
    b. To explain how a landlord should conduct himself in order to be successful.
    c. To illustrate how his kindness eased the family's adaptation to their new home and circumstances.
    d. To demonstrate that he did not need to be cold and businesslike all of the time.

8. At the start of paragraph two, the narrator refers to the Dashwoods' new home as being "defective." What does the narrator mean?
    a. The tall hills surround and hide the home from neighboring structures.
    b. The building is much too poor and crowded for the family.
    c. The home's insufficiently sized parlors are too small for entertaining.
    d. The building's look and feel do not resemble that of a typical cottage.

9. Which of the following best describes the tone of the passage?
    a. Melancholy
    b. Inventive
    c. Upbeat
    d. Apprehensive

10. Toward the end of paragraph six, the narrator says, "his entreaties were carried to a point of perseverance beyond civility." What does the narrator accomplish by saying this?
    a. Signifies the Dashwoods' annoyance with the fake friendliness of Sir John Middleton
    b. Describes Sir John Middleton's slightly overbearing, overly effusive invitations
    c. Demonstrates the language from the time period in which the piece was penned
    d. Questions the genuineness of the offer for the family to stay at Barton Cottage

Passage II: Social Science

The following passage is taken from the Advantages of Division of Labor section in Chapter VI of Principles of Political Economy, by John Stuart Mill:

The causes of the increased efficiency given to labor by the division of employments are some of them too familiar to require specification; but it is worthwhile to attempt a complete enumeration of them. By Adam Smith they are reduced to three: "First, the increase of dexterity in every particular workman; secondly, the saving of the time which is commonly lost in passing from one species of work to another; and, lastly, the invention of a great number of machines which facilitate and abridge labor, and enable one man to do the work of many."

(1.) Of these, the increase of dexterity of the individual workman is the most obvious and universal. It does not follow that because a thing has been done oftener it will be done better. That depends on the intelligence of the workman, and on the degree in which his mind works along with his hands. But it will be done more easily. This is as true of mental operations as of bodily. Even a child, after much practice, sums up a column of figures with a rapidity which resembles intuition. The act of speaking any language, of reading fluently, of playing music at sight, are cases as remarkable as they are familiar. Among bodily acts, dancing, gymnastic exercises, ease and brilliancy of execution on a musical instrument, are examples of the rapidity and facility acquired by repetition. In simpler manual operations the effect is, of course, still sooner produced.

(2.) The second advantage enumerated by Adam Smith as arising from the division of labor is one on which I can not help thinking that more stress is laid by him and others than it deserves. To do full justice to his opinion, I will quote his own exposition of it: "It is impossible to pass very quickly from one kind of work to another, that is carried on in a different place, and with quite different tools. A country weaver, who cultivates a small farm, must lose a good deal of time in passing from his loom to the field, and from the field to his loom. When the two trades can be carried on in the same workhouse, the loss of time is no doubt much less. It is even in this case, however, very considerable. A man commonly saunters a little in turning his hand from one sort of employment to another." I am very far from implying that these considerations are of no weight; but I think there are counter-considerations which are overlooked. If one kind of muscular or mental labor is different from another, for that very reason it is to some extent a rest from that other; and if the greatest vigor is not at once obtained in the second occupation, neither could the first have been indefinitely prolonged without some relaxation of energy. It is a matter of common experience that a change of occupation will often afford relief where complete repose would otherwise be necessary, and that a person can work many more hours without fatigue at a succession of occupations, than if confined during the whole time to one. Different occupations employ different muscles, or different energies of the mind, some of which rest and are refreshed while others work. Bodily labor itself rests from mental, and conversely. The variety itself has an invigorating effect on what, for want of a more philosophical appellation, we must term the animal spirits—so important to the efficiency of all work not mechanical, and not unimportant even to that.

(3.) The third advantage attributed by Adam Smith to the division of labor is, to a certain extent, real. Inventions tending to save labor in a particular operation are more likely to occur to any one in proportion as his thoughts are intensely directed to that occupation, and continually employed upon it.

This also can not be wholly true. "The founder of the cotton manufacture was a barber. The inventor of the power-loom was a clergyman. A farmer devised the application of the screw-propeller. A fancy-goods shopkeeper is one of the most enterprising experimentalists in agriculture. The most remarkable architectural design of our day has been furnished by a gardener. The first person who supplied London with water was a goldsmith. The first extensive maker of English roads was a blind man, bred to no trade. The father of English inland navigation was a duke, and his engineer was a millwright. The first great builder of iron bridges was a stone-mason, and the greatest railway engineer commenced his life as a colliery engineer."

(4.) The greatest advantage (next to the dexterity of the workmen) derived from the minute division of labor which takes place in modern manufacturing industry, is one not mentioned by Adam Smith, but to which attention has been drawn by Mr. Babbage: the more economical distribution of labor by classing the work-people according to their capacity.

11. Which of the following statements would the author agree is an advantage associated with the division of labor proposed by Adam Smith?
    a. Dexterity increases as employees complete repeated tasks
    b. Repetition results in increased monotony for employees
    c. Greater interdependence forms in the production process
    d. Unemployment increases as workers are replaced by machines

12. In paragraph five, why does the author mention that the "first great builder of iron bridges was a stone-mason"?
    a. To provide an example of how a person can do anything that he or she sets his or her mind to
    b. To demonstrate that Adam Smith's third advantage associated with the division of labor is not entirely true
    c. To explain that individuals are not always employed in professions for which they have received schooling
    d. To state that it is possible for individuals to have more than one career during their working life

13. Which statement best expresses the passage's main idea?
    a. The effect of specialization of division of labor
    b. Disproving the economic principles of Adam Smith
    c. Advantages associated with the division of labor
    d. Basic principles of macroeconomics

14. Which advantage associated with the division of labor does the author say is the second most important one?
    a. Increase of dexterity in employees
    b. Savings of time by staying on one type of work
    c. Invention of machines to assist with manual labor
    d. Classification of employees by their abilities

15. In paragraph two of this passage, what does the word "bodily" mean?
    a. Tangible
    b. Animal
    c. Organic
    d. Spiritual

16. Which word best describes the author's attitude toward Adam Smith?
    a. Dismissive
    b. Respectful
    c. Adoring
    d. Questioning

17. Based on the second advantage mentioned in the passage, what would be the most efficient course of action for an employee working in a copy center?
    a. The employee should focus on only a single task, such as producing black and white copies for large company orders.
    b. The employee should produce copies in one room and then go to a different building hall to collate and bind documents.
    c. The employee should produce black and white copies for a few hours and then change their focus to shipping out copy orders to customers.
    d. The employee should be allowed unlimited flexibility to schedule their daily work tasks however they see fit.

18. Which idea is supported by this passage?
    a. Repetitive tasks lead to stability in employees' work.
    b. One employee should complete all of the tasks in a workflow.
    c. Electronic toll collection is taking jobs from workers.
    d. Milking machines help to speed up the retrieval of milk from dairy farms.

19. A doll manufacturer opens a new facility and needs employees who can cut fabric, stuff bodies, and make delicate hair and facial features. Instead of hiring employees and cross-training them on all the tasks, the manufacturer hires staff with varying degrees of skill for the various tasks. What is this is an example of?
    a. Classing employees by their capacity
    b. Increasing dexterity by training on repetitive tasks
    c. Exclusively hiring experienced employees
    d. Introducing machines to assist with unfamiliar tasks

20. In paragraph three of this passage, why does the author use the phrase "animal spirits"?
    a. To provide an example of how employees feel when they work beyond fatigue
    b. To explain the positive effect that variety in work has on employees
    c. To demonstrate how employees feel when they do not receive proper training
    d. To state how employees are aversely affected when they change tasks

Passage III (A and B): Humanities

Passage A
The following passage is taken from Compassion and Benevolence under The Affections in Section II Of
The Philosophy of the Moral Feelings, by John Abercrombie, M.D. OXON. & EDIN:

The exercise of the benevolent affections may be briefly treated of, under nearly the same heads
as those referred to when considering the principle of Justice;—keeping in mind that they lead
to greater exertion for the benefit of others, and thus often demand a greater sacrifice of self-
love, than is included under the mere requirements of justice. On the other hand, benevolence is
not to be exercised at the expense of Justice; as would be the case, if a man were found relieving
distress by such expedients as involve the necessity of withholding the payment of just debts, or
imply the neglect or infringement of some duty which he owes to another.

(1.) Compassion and benevolent exertion are due toward alleviating the distresses of others. This
exercise of them, in many instances, calls for a decided sacrifice of personal interest, and, in
others, for considerable personal exertion. We feel our way to the proper measure of these
sacrifices, by the high principle of moral duty, along with that mental exercise which places us in
the situation of others, and, by a kind of reflected self-love, judges of the conduct due by us to
them in our respective circumstances.—The details of this subject would lead us into a field too
extensive for our present purpose. Pecuniary aid, by those who have the means, is the most easy
form in which benevolence can be gratified, and that which often requires the least, if any,
sacrifice of personal comfort or self-love. The same affection maybe exercised in a degree much
higher in itself, and often much more useful to others, by personal exertion and personal
kindness. The former, compared with the means of the individual, may present a mere mockery of
mercy; while the latter, even in the lowest walks of life, often exhibit the brightest displays of
active usefulness that can adorn the human character. This high and pure benevolence not only is
dispensed with willingness, when occasions present themselves; but seeks out opportunities for
itself, and feels in want of its natural and healthy exercise when deprived of an object on which it
may be bestowed.

(2.) Benevolence is to be exercised toward the reputation of others. This consists not only in
avoiding any injury to their characters, but in exertions to protect them against the injustice of
others,—to correct misrepresentations,—to check the course of slander, and to obviate the efforts
of those who would poison the confidence of friends, or disturb the harmony of society.

Passage B
The following passage is taken from Part II in Section II Of Benevolence in An Enquiry Concerning the
Principles of Morals, by David Hume:

Giving alms to common beggars is naturally praised; because it seems to carry relief to the
distressed and indigent: but when we observe the encouragement thence arising to idleness and
debauchery, we regard that species of charity rather as a weakness than a virtue.

Tyrannicide, or the assassination of usurpers and oppressive princes, was highly extolled in
ancient times; because it both freed mankind from many of these monsters, and seemed to keep
the others in awe, whom the sword or poignard could not reach. But history and experience
having since convinced us, that this practice increases the jealousy and cruelty of princes, a
Timoleon and a Brutus, though treated with indulgence on account of the prejudices of their
times, are now considered as very improper models for imitation.

Liberality in princes is regarded as a mark of beneficence, but when it occurs, that the homely bread of the honest and industrious is often thereby converted into delicious cates for the idle and the prodigal, we soon retract our heedless praises. The regrets of a prince, for having lost a day, were noble and generous: but had he intended to have spent it in acts of generosity to his greedy courtiers, it was better lost than misemployed after that manner.

Luxury, or a refinement on the pleasures and conveniences of life, had not long been supposed the source of every corruption in government, and the immediate cause of faction, sedition, civil wars, and the total loss of liberty. It was, therefore, universally regarded as a vice, and was an object of declamation to all satirists, and severe moralists. Those, who prove, or attempt to prove, that such refinements rather tend to the increase of industry, civility, and arts regulate anew our MORAL as well as POLITICAL sentiments, and represent, as laudable or innocent, what had formerly been regarded as pernicious and blamable.

Upon the whole, then, it seems undeniable, THAT nothing can bestow more merit on any human creature than the sentiment of benevolence in an eminent degree; and THAT a PART, at least, of its merit arises from its tendency to promote the interests of our species, and bestow happiness on human society. We carry our view into the salutary consequences of such a character and disposition; and whatever has so benign an influence, and forwards so desirable an end, is beheld with complacency and pleasure. The social virtues are never regarded without their beneficial tendencies, nor viewed as barren and unfruitful. The happiness of mankind, the order of society, the harmony of families, the mutual support of friends, are always considered as the result of their gentle dominion over the breasts of men.

21. According to the author of passage A, which example of benevolence is the simplest to execute?
    a. Providing money to enable a student the opportunity to attend an educational workshop
    b. Holding a lemonade stand to raise funds and awareness for pediatric cancer
    c. Shopping for new toys to donate to a fundraiser that collects gifts for needy kids
    d. Volunteering to cook and serve Thanksgiving dinner for homeless people

22. In paragraph two of passage A, what kind of "mental exercise" does the author discuss?
    a. Practicing to improve an individual's recall from memory
    b. Trying to see things from another person's point of view
    c. Strengthening a person's ability to concentrate and focus
    d. Taking only a singular perspective into consideration

23. In paragraph one of passage A, what does the term "heads" mean?
    a. Discord
    b. Unlikeness
    c. Manner
    d. Opposition

24. According to passage A, which statement accurately reflects the relationship between benevolence and justice?
    a. Benevolence can be exercised at the expense of justice
    b. Acts of justice require selflessness
    c. Benevolence can be offered in lieu of payment of debts
    d. Justice can be exercised at the expense of benevolence

25. Why does the author of passage B say that giving food and money to beggars is seen as a weakness?
    a. That type of charity encourages laziness and corruption
    b. Some individuals are not truly deserving of the charity
    c. The grants cannot reach all who are affected by poverty
    d. Individuals refuse to accept the handouts due to their pride

26. In paragraph five of passage B, the author uses the phrase "their gentle dominion over the breasts of men." What has dominion over the breasts of men, according to the author?
    a. Merit
    b. The sentiment of benevolence
    c. The social virtues
    d. Complacency and pleasure

27. Which word best describes the author's attitude toward luxury in passage B?
    a. Adoring
    b. Nostalgic
    c. Objective
    d. Dismissive

28. Which statement best describes the way the two passages use point of view?
    a. Passage A is written in second-person point of view, and passage B is written in third-person objective point of view.
    b. Passage A is written in first-person point of view, and passage B is written in third-person objective point of view.
    c. Passage A is written in third-person objective point of view, and passage B is written in third-person limited omniscient point of view.
    d. Passage A is written in first-person point of view, and passage B is written in first-person point of view.

29. Which of the following statements best explains the difference in the tones of the passages?
    a. The tone of passage A is objective, and the tone of passage B is earnest.
    b. The tone of passage A is cynical, and the tone of passage B is sarcastic.
    c. The tone of passage A is excited, and the tone of passage B is ambivalent.
    d. The tone of passage A is sarcastic, and the tone of passage B is cynical.

30. The author of passage B stresses the importance of exercising benevolence for which purpose?
    a. Reducing the suffering of another person
    b. Contributing to the overall happiness of society
    c. Preventing damage to someone else's good name
    d. Attracting good karma to oneself and others

Passage IV: Natural Science

The following passage is taken from the Muscles, Tendons, and Tendon Sheaths section in Chapter XVIII of <u>Manual of Surgery</u>, by Alexis Thomson, F.R.C.S.ED. and Alexander Miles, F.R.C.S. ED.:

Tendon sheaths have the same structure and function as the synovial membranes of joints and are liable to the same diseases. Apart from the tendon sheaths displayed in anatomical dissections, there is a loose peritendinous and perimuscular cellular tissue that is subject to the same pathological conditions as the tendon sheaths proper.

Tenosynovitis. The toxic or infective agent is conveyed to the tendon sheaths through the bloodstream, as in the gouty, gonorrheal, and tuberculous varieties, or is introduced directly through a wound, as in the common pyogenic form of tenosynovitis.

Tenosynovitis crepitans: In the simple or traumatic form of tenosynovitis, although the most prominent etiological factor is a strain or overuse of the tendon, there would appear to be some other, probably a toxic, factor in its production; otherwise the affliction would be much more common than it is: only a small proportion of those who strain or overuse their tendons become the subjects of tenosynovitis. The opposed surfaces of the tendon and its sheath are covered with fibrinous lymph, so that there is friction when they move on one another.

The *clinical features* are pain on movement, tenderness on pressure over the affected tendon, and a sensation of crepitation or friction when the tendon is moved in its sheath. The crepitation may be soft like the friction of snow, or may resemble the creaking of new leather—"saddle-back creaking." There may be swelling in the long axis of the tendon, and redness and edema of the skin. If there is an effusion of fluid into the sheath, the swelling is more marked and crepitation is absent. There is little tendency to the formation of adhesions.

In the upper extremity, the sheath of the long tendon of the biceps may be affected, but the condition is most common in the tendons about the wrist, particularly in the extensors of the thumb, and it is most frequently met with in those who follow occupations which involve prolonged use or excessive straining of these tendons—for example, washerwomen or riveters. It also occurs as a result of excessive piano-playing, fencing, or rowing.

At the ankle it affects the peronei, the extensor digitorum longus, or the tibialis anterior. It is most often met with in relation to the tendo-calcaneus—*Achillo-dynia*—and results from the pressure of ill-fitting boots or from the excessive use and strain of the tendon in cycling, walking, or dancing. There is pain in raising the heel from the ground, and creaking can be felt on palpation.

The *treatment* consists in putting the affected tendon at rest, and with this object a splint may be helpful; the usual remedies for inflammation are indicated: Bier's hyperemia, lead and opium fomentations, and ichthyol and glycerin. The affliction readily subsides under treatment, but is liable to relapse on a repetition of the exciting cause.

Gouty tenosynovitis: A deposit of urate of soda beneath the endothelial covering of tendons or of that lining their sheaths is commonly met with in gouty subjects. The accumulation of urates may result in the formation of visible nodular swellings, varying in size from a pea to a cherry, attached to the tendon and moving with it. They may be merely unsightly, or they may interfere with the use of the tendon. Recurrent attacks of inflammation are prone to occur. We have removed such gouty masses with satisfactory results.

Suppurative tenosynovitis: This form usually follows upon infected wounds of the fingers—especially of the thumb or little finger—and is a frequent sequel to whitlow; it may also follow amputation of a finger. Once the infection has gained access to the sheath, it tends to spread, and may reach the palm or even the forearm, being then associated with cellulitis. In moderately acute cases the tendon and its sheath become covered with granulations, which subsequently lead to the formation of adhesions; while in more acute cases the tendon sloughs. The pus may burst into the cellular tissue outside the sheath, and the suppuration is liable to spread to neighbouring sheaths or to adjacent bones or joints—for example, those of the wrist.

The *treatment* consists in inducing hyperemia and making small incisions for the escape of pus. The site of incision is determined by the point of greatest tenderness on pressure. After the inflammation has subsided, active and passive movements are employed to prevent the formation of adhesions between the tendon and its sheath. If the tendon sloughs, the dead portion should be cut away, as its separation is extremely slow and is attended with prolonged suppuration.

31. Which statement best expresses the main idea of the passage?
    a. A discussion of the causes, symptoms, and treatments associated with various types of tenosynovitis
    b. The similarities that exist between tendon sheaths and the synovial membranes of joints
    c. An exploration of sports and professions that may be responsible for injuries to tendons
    d. Differences in how tenosynovitis displays in injuries of the wrist versus injuries of the ankle

32. According to the passage, which of the following is a treatment for tenosynovitis crepitans of the ankle?
    a. Depositing urate of soda under the endothelial tendon covering
    b. Placing the tendon at rest, possibly utilizing a splinting device
    c. Incorporating active and passive movements to prevent tendon adhesions
    d. Inducing hyperemia and making small incisions to release pus

33. Which statement is supported by the information in the third paragraph?
    a. Tenosynovitis crepitans directly results from the overuse of a tendon.
    b. Edema and redness of the skin will return a diagnosis of tenosynovitis crepitans.
    c. Since few overuse injuries result in tenosynovitis crepitans, a toxic agent may be at play.
    d. A dancer who strains a tendon will undoubtedly suffer from tenosynovitis crepitans.

34. According to the author, a patient having which of the following clinical features would be presenting with a case of Tenosynovitis crepitans?
    a. Visible nodular swellings
    b. Cellulitis infections
    c. Finger wound infections
    d. Sensation of friction

35. The authors' point of view in this passage can be described as which of the following?
    a. First-person
    b. Second-person
    c. Third-person limited omniscient
    d. Third-person objective

36. According to the passage, which of the following may be the end result of an infected wound of the finger?
    a. The formation of cellulitis
    b. Pus spreading to adjacent bones and joints of the wrist
    c. Amputation of the finger
    d. Formation of granules on tendons and sheaths

37. In paragraph four, the authors use the phrases "soft like the friction of snow" and "resemble the creaking of new leather" to describe which of the following?
    a. Pain and pressure due to an increase in movement
    b. Swelling in the long axis of the tendon
    c. Friction associated with tendon movement in the sheath
    d. Effusion of fluid in the sheath of the tendon

38. A construction worker is wearing work boots that are too tight, and he experiences pain when he lifts his heel. Based on the passage, he will most likely be diagnosed with which of the following?
    a. Tenosynovitis
    b. Suppurative tenosynovitis
    c. Gouty tenosynovitis
    d. Tenosynovitis crepitans

39. Why do the authors of this passage incorporate the words "washerwomen" and "riveters" in paragraph five?
    a. To give examples of repetitive motion jobs that may result in tenosynovitis crepitans
    b. To emphasize the importance of healthcare for blue-collar workers
    c. To provide illustrations of recurrent inflammation attacks common to gouty tenosynovitis
    d. To illustrate why ergonomics in the workplace is essential to the health of employees

40. A woman presents to her physician's office with a nodular swelling on her thumb the size of a blueberry. Based on the passage, which condition will she most likely be diagnosed with?
    a. Tendo-calcaneus
    b. Gouty tenosynovitis
    c. Suppurative tenosynovitis
    d. Tenosynovitis

Answer Explanations #1

English

1. B: The underlined portion of this sentence is a preposition. Prepositions connect an object to nouns, to pronouns, or to a phrase representing a noun. Here, the noun is "view," Hawthorne's tragic view, and the object is "the literature of the United States." The preposition is the word "in," which indicates the vision is already within the body of literature. But the beginning of the sentence makes it clear that Hawthorne's vision is a new addition, so the correct preposition is "to," to show possession (the literature now includes Hawthorne's vision). "From" is incorrect because it is the opposite of "to," and "with" is incorrect because it signals that Hawthorne and the literature are co-contributors.

2. C: Collective nouns denote a group as a single unit, and they typically take a singular pronoun ("Mankind had its finest hour.") In this passage, "man" is taken as the universal, collective subject. "His" agrees with "man" and in this context is grammatically correct. Choice *B* ("her") would make the valid point that traditional constructs unfairly exclude women, but that argument is irrelevant to the discussion of Hawthorne's allegory of the human heart. Choice *D*, people's, is grammatically correct, but it is not the best choice, because the sentence is already about one collective subject, "man," and does not need another collective term, "people."

3. D: Choice *D* is a singular possessive noun. Choice *B* is the plural possessive of "humanities," the branches of learning. Choice C, "humanitys," is not a word.

4. A: The highlighted portion is an example of two independent clauses held together by a semicolon. The first clause is "but a few feet in, the light dims and warmth turns to chill," and the second one is "the visitor stumbles first in confusion, then in terror." The introductory phrase "but a few feet in" is an absolute phrase and must end with a comma. Inserting a comma after "dims" is inappropriate because the conjunction "and" connects only two actions. In the second clause, the comma after "confusion" substitutes for the conjunction "and." Choice B is incorrect because the comma separates the noun "light" from its verb "dims." Choice C is incorrect because the commas are needed to separate the phrases within the clauses. Choice *D* is incorrect because it lacks the appropriate commas and because the clause following the colon does not introduce a summary or an explanation.

5. D: "Farther" indicates additional distance, whereas "further" indicates an additional amount of something abstract, such as time. Choice *B* interrupts the sense of journey the writer is describing, and therefore is not the best answer. Choice *C* is awkward; "toward" rather than "to" is correct.

6. C: Choice *C* is correct because a colon is used to introduce a summary or an explanation. The phrase "the beauty that lies beyond fear and hopelessness" further describes Hawthorne's vision of human nature. Choice *B* is incorrect because it is a fragment, not a complete sentence. Choice *D* is incorrect because parentheses are used to enclose nonessential elements such as minor digressions.

7. B: Choice *B* is correct because inserting the article "an" creates parallel construction with "a natural morality." Choices *C* and *D* are incorrect because they lack parallel construction.

8. D: The word "affect" is a verb that means "to have an influence on," whereas "effect" in this sentence is a noun synonymous with "result." Choices *B* and *C* are incorrect because they alter the writer's intended meaning.

9. B: While Choices *A*, *C*, and *D* might all describe the moral setting of New England's Puritan community, Choice *B* is the closest synonym to "rigid."

10. A: Choice *A* is correct, because the passage indicates salvation is earned by an individual through right actions. It is not given (Choice *B*), bought (Choice *C*), or taken (Choice *D*).

11. D: The placement of commas changes the meaning in this passage. This passage says a person must pay for their sins by themselves. Therefore the word "individual" modifies an isolation that takes place on spiritual, psychological, and physical planes. Choice *B* is incorrect because without commas, there is no way to be certain of the writer's intention. Choice *C* is incorrect because in it "individual" is used as an adjective, along with "spiritual," "psychological," and "physical."

12. B: Choice *A* is to the point, but in its brevity, it loses the idea of progression. Choice *C* is confusing because there is not enough information given about the awakening itself. Is it a physical awakening, or perhaps a spiritual one? Choice *D* includes all the information in the underlined passage, but is equally wordy. Choice *B* is the best choice because it states the action in a clear, straightforward fashion.

13. A: The coordinating conjunction "nor" pairs with "neither," as "or" pairs with "either." Choice *B* is incorrect because it states the opposite of what is in the underlined passage. Choices *C* and *D* are incorrect because they do not reflect the writer's intention.

14. C: Choices *A*, *B*, and *D* are all true statements, but they do not connect the underlined passage 13 to underlined passage 14. The correct answer is Choice *C* because it describes how Hawthorne arrived at the results reported in underlined passage 14.

15. B: Choice *B* is correct. It could be argued that the conclusion (Choice *C*) and the novel (Choice *D*) both contain light and shadows, but the essay is about Hawthorne's allegory of the human heart as a cave holding both light and shadows; it is most fitting that Hester's heart be described that way.

16. C: The correct answer is Choice *C* because the phrase "which took place between 1760 and 1840" is set off with commas. Choice *B* is incorrect because it lacks a comma after "1840," and Choice *D* is incorrect because the comma after "place" interrupts the phrase "took place between 1760 and 1840."

17. D: Choice *B* is incorrect because a word is missing: that. The phrase should be "problems *that* threatened European society." Choice *C* is incorrect because it is awkward and confusing. Choice *D* is the correct answer because it uses "that," which does not take a preceding comma, as "which" must.

18. D: Choice *D*, "transformed," is the most accurate substitution because the essay describes the dramatic demographic changes that happened to European society during the Industrial Revolution. Choice *A* ("transfigured") suggests a radical change in figure or appearance, and as such is less exact than "transformed." Choice *B* ("disrupted") does not convey the idea of change, and Choice *C* ("destroyed") is inaccurate because the existing social order was not destroyed.

19. C: The correct answer is Choice *C* because it includes the missing word "as" ("digging *as* deeply"). Choices *A*, *B*, and *D* are incorrect because they do not include the missing word.

20. A: Choice *B*, "indelible," is incorrect because it means permanent. Although industrialization did become permanent, the paragraph is outlining the development of industrialization, not proving its permanence. Choice *C* ("inadvertent") erroneously implies that industrialization was accidental or unintentional. Choice *D* ("inadvisable") classifies industrialization as "unwise," and that thought is not in line with this story of how industrialization developed.

21. A: Choice *A* is the best selection, because it provides the link from the expense of building factories to the capitalists, which led to industry becoming the new source of wealth. Choice *B* is awkwardly worded, and although it correctly states the need for capitalists, it does not put them into action. Choice *C* is factually correct, but is not the best choice because the tone is more casual than that of the rest of the essay. Choice *D* is factually incorrect and contradicts information supplied earlier in the paragraph: supply, demand, and markets existed before the Industrial Revolution.

22. B: Choice *B* is the clearest rewrite. Forming two sentences allows for linear sequencing of the activities.

23. A: Choice *A* is the correct answer. "Amount" refers to items that cannot be counted, whereas "number" refers to something, such as people, that can be counted.

24. C: Choice *C* is the correct answer because it uses past tense ("had"), which is consistent with the rest of the paragraph.

25. D: In a simple sentence such as the underlined passage, there is no need for a comma before the coordinating conjunction "and." Choice *B* is incorrect because with the semicolon, the second half of the sentence becomes a fragment. Choice *C* is incorrect because the conjunction is set off by two commas.

26. A: The correct answer is Choice *A*. Choice *B* ("impounded") indicates the children were seized and confined. If the children were apprenticed (Choice *C*), they would have been legally bound to a tradesman or craftsman to work for a specific amount of time in exchange for learning a skill. If they were conscripted (Choice *D*), they would have been forced into military service.

27. D: Following the rules of Who, What, Where, When, and Why, the children worked in factories for thirteen hours a day, six days a week. The reason Why can be given at the beginning of the sentence, as is the case here, or at the end. Choices *A*, *B*, and *C* are incorrect because Where follows When, and Choice *C* is further incorrect because it assumes that the day off was always a Sunday.

28. D: Choice *A* is incorrect because "beaten, kicked and bruised by overseers" is one item of the list of cruelties the children faced, yet the placement the phrase blurs it together with "heat and cold." Choice *B* is incorrect because the conjunction "and" is set off by two commas. Choice *C* is incorrect because a comma should follow "overseers," to enclose the treatment at the hands of the overseers as one item. Choice *D* is correct because incorporating the "extreme heat and cold" item into the main clause of the sentence allows "beaten, kicked, and bruised by overseers" to stand as one item delineated by commas.

29. D: The summary lists lack of education as a problem that was either created or aggravated by the Industrial Revolution, but there is no mention of education in the essay.

30. C: The introduction lists three problem areas—economic, social, and political—but the essay discusses only economic and social challenges.

31. B: While cardiologists (Choice *C*) and the American Obesity Association (Choice *D*) are actively dealing with the obesity epidemic in the United States, this paragraph focuses on a hospital's response. The correct answer is Choice *B*, "facilities." Choice *A* is incorrect because the closest definition of "faculties" that might fit in this context is "teachers and instructors in branches of learning in a college or university." If the writer had intended to use "faculties," they would have identified which branch, such as "medical faculties."

32. A: The spelling and punctuation are correct as written (Choice *A*). Choice *B* lacks a comma between the town and the state, as well as a comma after the state, to enclose the clause. In Choice *C*, Massachusetts is misspelled, and if Choice *D* were used, the essay would then contain less factual information than the original.

33. B: "BMI's" is incorrect because it is the possessive form of "BMI." Choice *B* ("BMIs) is correct because it is the plural form of "BMI." Choices *C* and *D* are incorrect because the acronym is spelled out in full; as it has already been introduced to the reader, it should be used here, not the full term.

34: C: Choice *C* is the correct answer because it states that sleep apnea *can* cause problems; the other choices imply that it always causes problems. In addition, Choices *B* and *D* each have an additional error. Choice B is written in the incorrect tense—it uses past tense instead of present tense. Choice *D* omits mentioning that the problems are caused during surgery.

35. C: Choice *A* is incorrect because in the underlined phrase "patients" is plural, indicating more than one patient. Choice *B* is incorrect because "patient" is positioned as a descriptive adjective, rather than as a noun. Choice *D* is partly correct because "patients'" is possessive, but it is incorrect because the word is in the plural form. Choice *C* is correct: it is the singular, possessive form of "patient."

36. A: This question involves proper placement of the adverb "only," which should precede the noun/verb combination it modifies, and it should also be as close to the combination as possible. The underlined phrase, as written, is correct. The device was not in the operating room on a regular basis; one was stocked if the staff knew in advance that the patient had a high BMI. The action being modified is the expectation of difficulty, therefore "only" precedes it and is as close as possible to the words "if difficulty was expected." Choice *B* is incorrect because the adverb follows the action statement. Choice *C* is incorrect because, by following directly behind "equipment," the word "only" attaches itself to that noun. Choice *D* is incorrect because the sentence does not make sense with that wording.

37. D: The correct answer is Choice *D*, "extended." Choices *A* ("unreasonable "), *B* ("outrageous "), and *C* ("unacceptable") are subjective and imply value judgments. "Extended," on the other hand, is factual and tells the reader specifically what it is about the amount of time that leads to rhabdomyolysis.

38. C: The comma before the conjunction "and" in Choice *A* makes this phrase grammatically incorrect. The same is true of Choice *B*. Choice *D* is incorrect because the dashes give the writing a jerky quality. Choice *C* is a simple statement of fact, does not contain a comma before the conjunction, and does not even need dashes.

39. A: A personal pronoun is needed in this phrase, and "their" (Choice *A*) is the correct one. As the reader is not told the patient's gender, the personal pronouns "his" and "her" would be incorrect, and "it" (Choice *D*) would not apply to a person. "They're" (Choice *B*) is a contraction of "they are," which does not make sense in this sentence. Choice *C* ("there") is an adverb, meaning "at, in, or to a place," which also makes no sense.

40. B: Choice *B*, "ensure" is the correct word. "Insure" (Choice *A*) relates to matters of legal and financial protection; "assure" (Choice *C*) means "to promise"; and "invalidate" (Choice *D*) contradicts what the writer is trying to say.

41. C: Choice *C*, "weight and height" is correct. The second sentence in the essay explains that BMI is determined by dividing height into weight.

42. B: The second paragraph discusses the special fiber-optic device that is needed in case there is a problem with intubation or delivering anesthesia, so the correct answer is Choice *B*.

43. C: The mattresses are called "pressure-relief" mattresses, which indicates their job is to address the problem of pressure, not patient comfort (Choice *A*), muscle relaxation (Choice *B*), or sleep (Choice *D*).

44. A: Choice *A* is the correct answer because while summarizing the paragraph, it also points back to the opening statement. Choice *B* is redundant in that the essay has already stated that the task force established the new protocol. Choice *C* initiates a new topic, which is the opposite of what a conclusion should do. Choice *D* states what should be an obvious reaction.

45. D: Choice *D* is best because it states three key points clearly and succinctly. Choice *A* is not the best choice because readers outside of the medical profession might not know what an early notification protocol is; Choice *B* is a bit misleading because it's the protocol, not the task force, that saves lives; and Choice *C* is vague because it does not specify what the success is or how it is being achieved.

46. D: "Afflicts" is an acceptable substitute for "affects," in the context of this sentence. Choices *A* (destroys") and *C* ("kills") are both incorrect choices because not everyone who is affected by a stroke is killed by it. Choice *B* ("effects") is not correct because it is a noun.

47. D: The key phrase in the underlined passage is "*risk* of stroke." The demographics show who in the population is prone to stroke, but they don't guarantee that those people will have strokes. Likewise, they don't guarantee that anyone falling outside of the categories listed will not have a stroke. The correct answer is Choice *D*. It is possible that Carlos might have a stroke in his lifetime.

48. C: Inserted at the end of the paragraph, the sentence about pseudobulbar affect is confusing because the disease has not been introduced yet, and so the reader has no context to put the comment in. The paragraph ends without any additional information that would justify the sentence being there. Choice *A* is incorrect because the information might be very relevant to the essay—but only if it is included in the correct place. Choice *B* is incorrect because the additional information does not support the topic sentence, "What exactly is a stroke?" Choice *D* is incorrect not because the statistic is relatively positive, but because stroke survival is not the topic of the sentence.

49. B: The logical order is the order in which the events occur, as presented in Choice *B*. The blood flow disruption begins, it can be disrupted for up to twenty-four hours, and death can be a result.

50. C: Choice *C*, "poles," is the closest synonym because as with extremes, poles lie at either end of the spectrum. Choice *A* ("spectrums") is incorrect because there is only one spectrum and it is the continuum of all possibilities that lie between the extremes, including the extremes. Choices *B* ("states") and *D* ("positions") do not connote the sense of opposites that "extremes" does.

51. B: Choice *B* is correct because the comma separates the main clause in the sentence from the subordinating clause. Choice *C* would be correct if there was a comma after "brain" as well. Choice *D* is incorrect because the comma interrupts the prepositional phrase "to CNS tissue."

52. B: The correct answer is Choice *B*. The paragraph discusses clots and plaque that form in the CNS, and clots and plaque that form elsewhere. "Locally" indicates a position in the CNS itself, whereas "a blood clot or atherosclerotic plaque develops elsewhere, such as the heart" indicates a position outside of the CNS.

53. B: A semicolon separates main clauses that are not joined by a coordinating conjunction, such as "and." Choice *B* breaks this long sentence into two main clauses, each of which can stand on its own as a complete sentence.

54. C: The correct answer is Choice *C*, the semicolon. Because there is a set of dashes later in the sentence, Choice *B* ("dash") won't work because dashes are used only in pairs, and adding one would make three. Choice *A* ("slash") is used to separate two options, not two parts of a sentence. A period, Choice *D*, would be appropriate only if the lowercase "t" in "there" appeared as a capital "T" in the sentence.

55. C: The sentence beginning, "Noncontrast computed tomography..." disrupts the flow of the paragraph by inserting a comment about imaging technology into a discussion of stroke symptoms.

56. A: The sentence is correct as written. Choice *B* would be correct only if a comma and the word "it" were inserted after "leaked" ("as the blood is leaked, it can destroy brain tissue"). Choice *C* ("as the blood is leaked, can destroy brain tissue") is incorrect because the pronoun "it" is missing before "can." Choice *D* is incorrect because the tense changes mid-sentence.

57. B: The outline of types and subtypes of stroke is:

I. Ischemic

      A. Thrombotic

      B. Embolic

II. Hemorrhagic

      A. Intracerebral

      B. Subarachnoid

58. C: The logical order is:

      1: Introduction of stroke and stroke demographics

      2: Definition of stroke

      4: Symptoms

      3: Two main types of stroke (ischemic and hemorrhagic); ischemic described

      5: Hemorrhagic described

      6: Structural damage in ischemic and hemorrhagic stroke

Choice *A* introduces ischemic and hemorrhagic stroke. It should discuss the types in that order, but it covers hemorrhagic first. Choice *B* discusses structural damage of both types of stroke before covering hemorrhagic stroke in detail. Choice *D* discusses demographics and symptoms of stroke before defining what stroke is, and so the definition of the topic is delivered three paragraphs into the essay.

59. C: The passage to be inserted discusses the pathophysiology of hemorrhagic stroke, so it belongs in the paragraph devoted entirely to hemorrhagic stroke, Paragraph Number 5 (Choice *C*).

60. A: Choice *A* is false; it states that every American who has a stroke (795,000) dies from it.

61. D: "Represented" is most accurate word. "Marked" (Choice *A*) describes what the triplets, triads, and trios do, rather than what they are—they mark, or flag, the concept of three-ness. Choice *B* ("earmarked") means "marked with an identifying symbol" and is an interesting choice, but not one that is as synonymous as "represented." Choice *C* ("included") is not grammatically correct.

62. B: "The notion of" should be deleted, because "The significance of three-ness..." is much more direct. "Of these cultures" (Choice *C*) is a necessary reference to the Indo-European societies. "Numerous" (Choice *D*) attests to the quantity of these events, and it is stronger than simply "abounds with events."

63. C: The error lies in Choice *C*. "Their" is the correct spelling of the possessive form of "they."

64. B: "Clearly and uniformly" is the closest substitute. Choice *A*, "discerningly and constantly," bears little similarity to the original pair aside from beginning with the same letters. Choice *C*, "definitely and evenly," is not immediately clear and would require explanation. In Choice *D*, "easily" is not a synonym of "distinctly."

65. A: "Dwellers" is the closest synonym to "inhabitants." Both are plural nouns and mean "people who reside in or inhabit a certain place." "Authors" (Choice *B*) are a subset of people who might be inhabiting place; "cultures" (Choice *C*) encompass more than just the people themselves living somewhere; and "persons" (Choice *D*) applies to a specific, small number of people.

66. B: Choice *B* is the correct answer. Style and tone are important aspects of essay writing, and writing that distracts the reader from the point being made is to be avoided. Readers know when a writer is trying too hard, as is the case here.

67. D: This sentence has three pieces of information: there are *two levels of significance* to the *concept of three-ness* that is *applied by the authors*. The reader already knows that the authors of the sagas are the people who are applying the concept of three, so that piece of information does not need to be repeated. Choice *D* is the only choice that omits mentioning the authors and has no flaws. Choice *A* erroneously replaces "in" with "to," which does not make the sentence any clearer. Choice *B* indicates that the application, not the significance, has two levels. Choice *C* is close to the correct answer, but it would be simpler if it did not include the authors.

68. C: If the new paragraph appeared before the final paragraph, the order of topics would flow logically:

- Introduction of concept of three
- First level of significance
- Second level of significance
- Dual purpose of three-ness
- How the application of three-ness evolved over time

69. A: Choice *A* is the clearest rewrite. It replaces the "not only...but also..." structure with two sentences that are relatively simple to comprehend. Choice *B*, in the interest of brevity, leaves out two concepts: tempo and balance. In Choice *C*, the conjunction "but," which means "on the contrary," throws the intended meaning of the passage into question. Choice *D* is written in the passive voice (the subject is the recipient of the action), which is less direct than the active voice.

70. D: A three-legged stool is the most appropriate of the choices. Choice *A* (drawing compass) won't work because drawing compasses have only two legs. Choice *B* (tricycle) connotes movement along with balance, and in addition to being anachronistic, the image might be a bit childish in the context of this essay. Choice *D*, a three-legged dog, is inappropriate because dogs are not naturally born with just three legs, and it is a tasteless analogy as well.

71. C: Choice *C* is correct. The sentence states that there are three levels of relevance, when in reality there are only two.

72. A: The introductory phrase "For instance" should be followed by a comma.

73. C: This information is imparted in the thesis sentence.

74. B: The essay fails to support, through explanation and examples, one of the tenets of the thesis statement.

75. D: The only numbers that were special to the saga authors were three and its multiples. The logic and symmetry of two and four are not discussed in the essay.

Reading

1. A: The point of view of the narrator of the passage can best be described as third-person omniscient. The narrator refers to the characters in the story by third-person pronouns: *he, it,* and *they.* The narrator also comes across as "all-knowing" (omniscient) by relating the information and feelings about all the characters (instead of just those of a single character). Second-person point of view would incorporate the second-person pronoun, *you.* First-person point of view would incorporate first-person pronouns: *I* and *we.* Finally, the third-person objective point of view would also refer to the characters in the story by third-person pronouns *he, it,* and *they.* However, the narrator would stay detached, only telling the story and not expressing what the characters feel and think.

2. B: The chronological order of these four events in the passage is as follows:

1. The servants joyfully cheered for the family.
2. Mrs. Dashwood discussed improvements to the cottage.
3. Elinor hung her drawings up in the sitting room.
4. Sir John Middleton stopped by for a visit.

3. C: In the course of this passage, the Dashwoods' attitude shifts. The narrator initially describes the family's melancholy disposition at the start of their journey from Norland. However, the narrator then describes their spirits beginning to lift and becoming more upbeat as they make their way through the scenic English countryside to their new home at Barton Cottage. Although the remaining answer choices may contain some partial truths (appreciation for the family's former privileged life and fear about the family's expedition), they do not accurately depict the narrator's theme throughout the entire passage. For example, the family did not express disdain for their new landlord or doubt their future ability to survive.

4. D: Reality versus expectations is a theme of this passage. Although Mrs. Dashwood expects her new financial circumstances to be trying, and the family expects to miss their former place of residence for quite some time, the Dashwoods seem to begin to adapt well with the help of Sir John Middleton, their generous new landlord. A theme of love conquers all is typically used in literature when a character overcomes an obstacle due to his or her love for someone. A theme of power of wealth is used in literature to show that money either accomplishes things or is the root of evil. Finally, a theme of wisdom of experience is typically used in literature to show that improved judgment comes with age.

5. A: The statement at the start of paragraph five in this passage signifies the family is going through a transition. The Dashwoods find themselves in a time of great transition as they learn to accept their family's demotion in social standing and their reduced income. The statement was not meant to signify that Mrs. Dashwood needs to obtain meaningful employment, that the family is going through a growth phase, or that the Dashwood children need to be concerned about the future.

6. B: The new landlord is a cousin to the Dashwoods. This accurately depicts their relationship. The new landlord was not a former social acquaintance, Mrs. Dashwood's father, or a long-time friend of the family.

7. C: The narrator describes the generosity of Sir John Middleton to explain how his kindness eased the family's adaptation to their new home and circumstances. He played a very important role in making the Dashwoods feel comfortable moving to Barton Cottage. The narrator did not describe Sir John Middleton's generosity to identify one of the many positive traits that a landlord should possess, to explain how a landlord should conduct himself in order to be successful, or to demonstrate that he did not need to be cold and businesslike all the time.

8. D: The narrator's reference to the Dashwood's new home as being "defective" means that the building's look and feel do not resemble that of a typical cottage. The narrator describes the building as being regular, with a tiled roof (rather than a thatched roof), with shutters that are not green, and with walls not covered with honeysuckles—all characteristics that a traditional cottage would possess. Although the other three answer choices are true statements about their new home and property, they do not relate to the narrator's statement that the new home is "defective."

9. C: The overall tone of the passage is upbeat. Although the passage begins with the family in a melancholy disposition at the start of their journey (and perhaps a bit apprehensive), their spirits begin to lift as they make their way through the scenic English countryside to Barton Cottage.

10. B: The narrator is describing how exuberantly Sir John Middleton expresses his pleasure at gaining the Dashwoods as tenants. Sir John Middleton is overjoyed to welcome his cousins to the cottage on his property, which he expresses through his words, gifts, and invitations to dine with him. He just goes a bit too far in demonstrating his delight, for which the Dashwoods forgive him. Sir John Middleton does not express any fake friendliness. The phrase was not used to demonstrate the language from the time period in which the piece was penned. Finally, Sir John Middleton's offer for the Dashwoods to stay at Barton Cottage is indeed genuine.

11. A: The author would agree that an advantage associated with the division of labor proposed by Adam Smith is that dexterity increases as employees complete repeated tasks. The remaining three answer choices are known disadvantages related to the division of labor concept.

12. B: The author mentions that the "first great builder of iron bridges was a stone-mason" in paragraph five in order to demonstrate how the third advantage associated with the division of labor proposed by Adam Smith is not entirely true. Even though the author agrees with Adam Smith that the invention of machines helps employees to save time, he does not agree that employees who are intimately involved in a daily routine of work come up with the ideas for those inventions (i.e., "the inventor of the power-loom was a clergyman," not a weaver). The remaining answer choices are not addressed by the author in the passage.

13. C: The passage's main idea is best expressed by the answer choice "advantages associated with the division of labor." The passage does not focus solely on the effect of specialization of labor, which consists of increasing productivity by dividing up larger tasks into smaller tasks to be completed by workers with specialized skills.. The passage is not concerned with disproving Adam Smith's economic principles. Finally, macroeconomics deals with the larger economy as a whole and topics such as interest rates and gross domestic product. Thus, macroeconomics is not discussed in this passage.

14. D: In paragraph six, the author lists classification of employees by their abilities as the second most important advantage associated with the division of labor. The author states that this is "the greatest advantage (next to the dexterity of the workmen)," which is not mentioned as an advantage by Adam Smith. The remaining three answer choices are listed in the passage as advantages associated with the division of labor. However, they are not listed by the author as being the second most important advantage.

15. A: The author uses the word "bodily" in the second paragraph to mean tangible. The author is referring to the hands-on acts of dancing, gymnastics, and playing musical instruments. The remaining three answer choices are also meanings of the word *bodily*. However, they do not fit the author's use of the word *bodily* in this passage.

16. B: The author's attitude toward Adam Smith in this passage can be best described as respectful. The author does not adore Adam Smith, nor does he question or dismiss him and his theory. However, the author expands on the advantages associated with the division of labor to add in his own points where appropriate, and he describes one additional advantage not mentioned by Adam Smith.

17. C: Based on the second advantage, the author would suggest the most efficient course of action for an employee working in a copy center would be to produce black and white copies for a few hours and then change their focus to shipping out copy orders to customers. This is where the author says that he differs from Adam Smith. He believes that there is a benefit to having an employee gain relief from experiencing a change of occupation (or tasks) throughout their work day. Therefore, the author would not suggest that the most efficient course of action is having an employee focus on only a single task (as Adam Smith believed). Completing tasks in different locations is an idea that both the author and Adam Smith would not agree with. They were both proponents of performing tasks in one same physical location to cut down on transfer time. Finally, the author does not mention granting an employee unlimited flexibility in scheduling their work tasks.

18. D: This passage supports the idea of milking machines being used to help speed up the retrieval of milk from dairy farms. This is related to the third advantage: inventions tend to save labor. The passage does not mention that repetitive tasks may lead to stability in employees' work. Although the author mentions there is a benefit to having an employee gain relief from experiencing a change of occupation (or tasks) throughout their work day, he does not state that one employee should complete all the tasks in a workflow. Finally, the passage does not mention the downside of inventions, which is that sometimes they result in a loss of employee jobs.

19. A: Staffing the doll factory is an example of classing employees by their capacity; staff will be hired based on their skills for the tasks that are involved with manufacturing dolls. There is no mention of training employees on repetitive tasks to increase their dexterity or exclusively hiring only experienced employees. Finally, there is also no mention of introducing machines to assist employees with unfamiliar tasks.

20. B: The author uses the phrase "animal spirits" in paragraph three to explain the positive effect that variety in work has on employees. This is one of the areas in which the author expands on one of Adam Smith's advantages of the division of labor. Adam Smith says that time can be saved if employees focus on one type of work. The author is not dismissing his claim. However, he mentions that some employees may instead benefit from changing the type of work that they do during the day, and such variety invigorates some employees' animal spirits. The remaining answer choices (working beyond fatigue, failing to receive proper training, and employees being adversely affected when they change tasks) are not mentioned in the passage.

21. A: Providing money to allow a student the opportunity to attend an educational workshop is the simplest way to do something benevolent, according to the author of passage A. In the second paragraph of the passage, the author states that pecuniary (or monetary) aid is the easiest form of benevolence and that it requires the least amount of sacrifice. The remaining answer choices would all involve much greater amounts of sacrifice.

22. B: The phrase "mental exercise" is used in paragraph two of passage A to represent trying to see things from another person's point of view. In paragraph two, the author is discussing practicing benevolence by placing oneself in the situations of others. The author does not make mention of a person only taking their own perspective into consideration, improving an individual's memory recall, or strengthening a person's concentration.

23. C: In passage A, the term "heads" means manner. The author is discussing treating the practice of benevolent affections in almost the same way or manner as when considering the principles of justice. The remaining answer choices (discord, unlikeness, and opposition) do not make sense in this context.

24. D: The author of passage A states that justice can be exercised at the expense of benevolence, but this premise is not true the other way around ("benevolence is not to be exercised at the expense of justice"). Additionally, acts of benevolence require selflessness (not acts of justice). Finally, benevolence cannot take the place of the payment of debts that are owed per acts of justice.

25. A: The author of passage B says that giving food and money to beggars is seen as a weakness because that type of charity encourages laziness and corruption ("giving alms to common beggars" leads to an increase in "idleness and debauchery"). Although the remaining answer choices may indeed be true, they are not mentioned by the author of passage B.

26. B: The phrase "their gentle dominion over the breasts of men" refers to the social virtues, compassion and benevolence. In this paragraph, the author discusses how the goal of benevolence is to promote the happiness of society. The other answer choices are mentioned in paragraph five, but the author does not propose they rule over people's inner spirits ("the breasts of men").

27. C: The author's attitude toward luxury in passage B can best be described as objective. The author is impartial and simply represents facts and attitudes about luxury. The author does not say luxury is unworthy of consideration (dismissive), does not think romantically or sentimentally about luxury (nostalgic), and does not worship luxury (adoring).

28. D: Both passage A and passage B are written in first-person point of view. The author uses the first-person plural pronouns *we* and *us*. Second-person point of view would use the second-person pronoun, *you*. Third-person objective point of view would utilize third-person pronouns: *he, she, it,* or *they*, and the author would stay detached by telling the story. Finally, third-person limited omniscient view would also use the third-person pronouns, and the author would tell the entire story through the eyes of a single character.

29. A: The tone of passage A is objective, and the tone of passage B is earnest. The author is passage A is uninfluenced by emotion, while the author of passage B shows deeper feelings with the incorporation of words in all capital letters and the phrases and examples which he selected. A cynical tone is used when an author is mocking others, and a sarcastic tone is used when an author wishes to state a negative opinion in an ironic way. Finally, an excited tone is used when an author is very happy about events, and an ambivalent tone is used when an author is unsure or undecided about something.

30. B: Compared to the author of passage A, the author of passage B stresses the importance of exercising benevolence for the purposes of contributing to the overall happiness of society ("bestow happiness on human society"). The author of passage A mentions the importance of uses benevolence to alleviate the distresses of others and to protect the reputations of others. The concept of attracting karma is not mentioned in either passage.

31. A: The main focus of the passage is a discussion of the causes, symptoms, and treatments associated with the various types of tenosynovitis. The remaining answer choices are all mentioned throughout the passage; however, they are separate, subordinate topics, not the main idea of the passage.

32. B: Placing the tendon at rest and possibly utilizing a splinting device is mentioned in the passage as a treatment for tenosynovitis crepitans of the ankle. Depositing urate of soda under the endothelial tendon covering is used to treat gouty tenosynovitis. Inducing hyperemia and making small incisions to release pus, as well as incorporating active and passive movements to prevent tendon adhesions, are both mentioned in the passage as treatments for suppurative tenosynovitis.

33. C: The statement is supported by the information found in the third paragraph, since the author states that only a small proportion of individuals who overuse their tendons are afflicted with the condition. This means that something else, such as the toxic factor that is mentioned, must be the reason.

34. D: According to the author, a patient having a sensation of crepitation or friction when the tendon is moved in its sheath would be presenting with a case of tenosynovitis crepitans. Visible nodular swellings are a clinical feature of gouty tenosynovitis. Finally, cellulitis and finger wound infections are both clinical features of suppurative tenosynovitis.

35. A: The authors use first-person point of view in this passage, which can be determined by the use of the first-person pronoun, *we*, in paragraph eight. Second-person point of view would involve the authors utilizing the second-person pronoun, *you*. Third-person limited omniscient view would involve the authors using third-person pronouns (*he, she, it*, or *they*), and the authors would tell the entire story through the eyes of a single character. Finally, third-person objective point of view would also involve the authors using the third-person pronouns: *he, she, it*, or *they*. However, the authors would stay detached and would not refer to themselves with the pronouns "I" or "we."

36. B: Pus spreading to the adjacent bones and joints of the wrist may be the end result of an infected wound of the finger, according to the passage. Based on the options provided, this answer choice would have the most finality for an individual suffering with this condition. The other answer choices are all complications that can result from an infected wound of the finger, but Choices *A* and *C* are not be as serious as the infection spreading from the finger to the bones and joints of the wrist. Choice *C*, amputation of the finger, is explicitly mention has a condition that can *precede* suppurative tenosynovitis, so it is not a good answer choice for an end result.

37. C: The phrases are used in paragraph four to describe the friction associated with tendon movement in the sheath. The authors utilize the phrases to express how the friction can present in varying degrees. Milder friction can be "soft like the friction of snow"; more intense friction can "resemble the creaking of new leather." The other answer choices are simply additional features of tenosynovitis crepitans.

38. D: The authors state in paragraph six that tenosynovitis crepitans at the ankle can result from the pressure of ill-fitting boots and that the individual affected would experience pain when raising his or her heels from the ground. Therefore, based on this passage, if a construction worker wearing tight boots experiences pain when raising his heel, he will more than likely be diagnosed with tenosynovitis crepitans.

39. A: The authors included the words "washerwomen" and "riveters" in paragraph five to give examples of workers whose repetitive motions on the job can result in tenosynovitis crepitans. The authors make no mention in the passage of the importance of healthcare for blue-collar workers or ergonomics in the workplace. Finally, the authors mention that recurrent attacks of inflammation are likely to occur in individuals suffering from gouty tenosynovitis. However, they do not provide any examples related to this in the passage.

40. B: Based on this passage, if a woman presents to her doctor with a nodular swelling on her thumb the size of a blueberry, she will more than likely be diagnosed with gouty tenosynovitis. This is the only affliction the authors mention is characterized by the formation of visible nodular swellings that vary in size from a pea to a cherry.

Practice Test #2

English

Questions 1–15 are based on the following passage:

The artwork produced in Christendom during the Middle Ages (410 (1) <u>CE</u> to 1266) was influenced to a great degree by the (2) <u>mideval</u> Christian Church, to which it owes not only its inspiration, but its preservation. The Church, being the most authoritative institution of the time, was a dominant influence on medieval art, effecting (3) <u>its</u> moral aspects of theme and purpose in addition to the technical ones of form and presentation. The art of the Dark Ages reflects the impact of the Church on social and political practice at the same time as it (4) <u>illuminated</u> the values and principles common to medieval man. To understand the properties of the art, it is essential to consider the religious philosophy that ruled the Middle Ages and influenced artistic tone.

(5) <u>Also known as the Dark Ages and the Medieval Era the period after the fall of the Roman Empire (the end of antiquity) and before the Renaissance (the rebirth of classical learning)</u> was a (6) <u>disjointed</u> time for Europe. Christianity, most specifically the Catholic Church, emerged as a unifying force, and Christian doctrine influenced all aspects of daily life. It replaced the traditions and learning of the ancient world with a new view of life, God, and (7) <u>mans</u> place in the world.

The Church taught Christians to believe in a God-centered universe in which man is weak and humble. To fill Europe's social void, the Church defined moral standards by (8) <u>lauding</u> humility, chastity, modesty, and poverty. It encouraged men and women to work for the cause of God, and it proclaimed the (9) <u>contemplation of and meditation on God</u> to be the most desirable of human activities.

The Pietistic art of the Dark Ages, mostly in the form of illuminated manuscripts, alter triptychs, and mosaics and frescoes in churches, fully embodies the doctrine of the Church. It most often depicts the holy family, saints, and scenes from the Bible, using iconography and color symbolism to represent abstract ideas and relate the stories in the Bible to people who could neither read nor write (10) <u>and at a time before printing existed</u>.

The point of the art of this time was to glorify God, rather than showcase (11) <u>aesthetic</u> sensibilities, and as a result, the human faces often appear flat, ill proportioned, and oddly alike. Faces show little to no emotion, and the (12) <u>baby</u> Jesus is often depicted with the face of an adult, looking as old as—if not older than—his mother, Mary. Figures are always fully clothed and often their posture is stiff and unrealistic looking. (13) <u>More concerned with conveying Christian beliefs and values, and showing respect to the Church, then with technical form, artists ignored perspective.</u> This can be seen in paintings of architecture and landscapes, where perspective is often distorted, and in scenes where important religious figures appear much larger than the figures around them.

(14) Because of its birth in an age of cultural stagnation—if not outright decline—, restricted subject matter, dark colors, and technical shortcomings, Christian art produced in the Middle Ages was for centuries judged by art historians and scholars alike to be inferior to the artwork created before it in the Classical period and afterward during the Renaissance, when appreciation for the skills and values of Classical art was "reborn." Only in the past century or so has medieval art come to be recognized as the foundation, and sometimes an underlying inspiration for, the (15) development of Western art.

1. Which is correct?
    a. NO CHANGE
    b. AD
    c. BC
    d. BDE

2. Which spelling is correct?
    a. NO CHANGE
    b. medeval
    c. medieval
    d. midevil

3. Which is correct?
    a. NO CHANGE
    b. it's
    c. its'
    d. their

4. Which is the most suitable choice to replace the underlined word?
    a. eliminated
    b. illuminates
    c. showed
    d. clarifies

5. A comma is missing from the sentence beginning with the word "also." Which choice correctly shows where the comma should be inserted?
    a. Also known as the Dark Ages and the Medieval Era, the period after the fall of the Roman Empire (the end of antiquity) and before the Renaissance (the rebirth of classical learning) was a disjointed time for Europe.
    b. Also known as the Dark Ages and the Medieval Era the period after the fall of the Roman Empire (the end of antiquity), and before the Renaissance (the rebirth of classical learning) was a disjointed time for Europe.
    c. Also, known as the Dark Ages and the Medieval Era the period after the fall of the Roman Empire (the end of antiquity) and before the Renaissance (the rebirth of classical learning) was a disjointed time for Europe.
    d. Also known as the Dark Ages and the Medieval Era the period after the fall of the Roman Empire (the end of antiquity) and before the Renaissance, (the rebirth of classical learning) was a disjointed time for Europe.

6. The definition of the underlined word is "having been taken apart at the joints," and it is not entirely appropriate in this context. Which choice is most accurate?
    a. disconnected
    b. upsetting
    c. disengaged
    d. unsettled

7. Which is correct?
    a. NO CHANGE
    b. mans'
    c. men's
    d. man's

8. Which, if any, of the following choices is the most accurate choice to replace the underlined word?
    a. praising
    b. applauding
    c. encouraging
    d. inspiring

9. The underlined phrase is awkward. Which choice makes the sentence easier to read?
    a. contemplation and meditation on God
    b. contemplation and meditation of God
    c. contemplation of, and meditation on, God
    d. contemplating and meditating on God

10. Why is the underlined phrase important?
    a. It helps to establish the time frame of the Dark Ages, for readers who do not know.
    b. It enforces the idea that not only couldn't most people read, there were no printed books for those who could.
    c. It points out just how backwards and dark the Dark Ages were.
    d. It shows what life was like before the printing press was invented.

11. Which change is correct?
    a. NO CHANGE
    b. technical
    c. ecstatic
    d. art-worthy

12. What is the closest synonym to the underlined word?
    a. lord
    b. infant
    c. savior
    d. child

13. Which replacement should be made in the underlined sentence?
    a. "Overly" should replace "more"
    b. "establishing" should replace "conveying"
    c. "than" should replace "then"
    d. "visual" should replace "technical"

14. The writer wants to shorten this long sentence that is full of subordinate clauses. Which choice could she eliminate without taking meaning away from the sentence?
    a. None of them can be eliminated.
    b. —if not outright decline—
    c. by art historians and scholars alike
    d. when appreciation for the skills and values of Classical art was "reborn"

15. Is there a concept mentioned in the first paragraph that isn't discussed elsewhere in the essay?
    a. No
    b. Yes, a description of the Middle Ages
    c. Yes, the ways in which art was preserved
    d. Yes, why the Church became so dominant

Questions 16–30 are based on the following passage:

(16) Glaucoma is a group of conditions that result in elevated intraocular pressure (IOP), damage to the optic nerve and retina, and a gradual, progressive loss of vision, frequently in both eyes. Peripheral vision is the first to be (17) effected, followed by central vision. (18) Because glaucoma often develops over a period of years and patients may not be aware that they have the disease due to a lack of symptoms in the early stages it is essential that (19) clinicians properly interpret the clinical presentation of the disease process. Two variables come into play with glaucoma: fluid drainage and intraocular pressure, (20) however it is important to note that IOP is not always a factor in the development of glaucoma.

Aqueous humor is a fluid that is produced behind the iris, in the posterior chamber of the eye. It drains by passing through the pupil to the (21) anterior chamber and leaves the eye through a multilayered tissue called the trabecular meshwork. Under normal conditions, most of the aqueous humor drains through the trabecular meshwork, but in glaucoma patients, (22) an alternative pathway called the uveoscleral pathway plays a role in drainage as well.

(23) When the aqueous humor does not drain properly (typically because an obstruction or increased resistance to outflow prevents the fluid from flowing out of the anterior chamber) IOP might increase to the point where damage can occur to the shape of the tissue around the head of the optic nerve and to the retina. (24) The mechanical stress and pressure on the sensitive tissues at the front of the eye can interfere with the function of the cells that transmit visual information in the form of electrical signals to the brain, negatively affecting vision.

The average IOP of the adult population in the United States is 16 mm Hg. Ocular hypertension (OHT) is the condition (25) in which IOP consistently measures above 21 mm Hg; patients with ocular hypertension have a higher risk of developing glaucoma.

Fundamental to understanding glaucoma, in particular the effects of high intraocular pressure on structures in the eye, is knowing the path the aqueous humor takes as it (26) flows through and out of the eye under normal conditions.

Both chambers of the eye—anterior and posterior—are filled with the aqueous humor. As noted above, normally aqueous humor is produced in the back of the eye and flows through the pupil to the front chamber, where it drains from the eye through conventional outflow channels. Specifically, it drains through the trabecular meshwork, which (27) comprises three layers of tissue, each layer containing tiny holes for the fluid to pass through. Then it passes through the canal of Schlemm and into other conventional pathways. In a healthy eye, approximately ninety percent of the aqueous fluid drains through the trabecular meshwork; the other ten percent leaves the eye by way of an unconventional passageway called the uveoscleral (28) <u>pathway (labeled "unconventional" because it is not a distinct pathway)</u>.

If, however, the flow of aqueous fluid from the anterior chamber is interrupted, pressure increases. In primary angle-closure glaucoma, increased pressure bows the iris into a convex shape until it touches the trabecular network, creating outflow resistance. (29) <u>When this happens and the conventional pathway is blocked the unconventional uveoscleral pathway takes on greater importance because uncontrolled increases in intraocular pressure can result in damage to the optic nerve, visual field loss, and even blindness</u>. (30)

16. If the underlined phrase is grammatically incorrect, which choice is correct?
   a. NO CHANGE
   b. Glaucoma is a group of conditions that results
   c. Glaucoma results
   d. Glaucoma is a condition that results

17. If the underlined word is used incorrectly, which choice is correct?
   a. NO CHANGE
   b. infected
   c. afflicted
   d. affected

18. This sentence has no internal punctuation. Which choice shows correct punctuation?
   a. Because glaucoma often develops over a period of years and patients may not be aware that they have the disease due to a lack of symptoms, in the early stages it is essential that clinicians properly interpret the clinical presentation of the disease process.
   b. Because glaucoma often develops over a period of years and patients may not be aware that they have the disease due to a lack of symptoms in the early stages, it is essential that clinicians properly interpret the clinical presentation of the disease process.
   c. Because glaucoma often develops over a period of years, and patients may not be aware that they have the disease due to a lack of symptoms in the early stages, it is essential that clinicians properly interpret the clinical presentation of the disease process.
   d. Because glaucoma often develops over a period of years, and patients may not be aware that they have the disease, due to a lack of symptoms, in the early stages, it is essential that clinicians properly interpret the clinical presentation of the disease process.

19. What is the closest substitute for the word "clinicians" in this passage?
   a. Eye surgeons
   b. Eye care professionals
   c. Optometrists
   d. Ophthalmologists

20. If the underlined word is used incorrectly, which choice is correct?
   a. NO CHANGE
   b. consequently
   c. but
   d. although

21. What is the meaning of the underlined word?
    a. Larger
    b. Smaller
    c. Foremost
    d. Rearmost

22. What is the best substitute for the underlined phrase?
    a. a connective
    b. an inferior
    c. an emergency
    d. an additional

23. If there is an error in the underlined sentence, which is it?
    a. "outflow prevents" should be "outflows prevents"
    b. There should be a comma immediately before "IOP might."
    c. "IOP might increase" should be "IOP may increase."
    d. The word "to" should be deleted from the phrase "and to the retina."

24. Which choice shows the error in the sentence?
    a. "front" should be "back"
    b. "function" should be "role"
    c. "transmit" should be "carry"
    d. "visual" should be "vital"

25. Which is correct?
    a. NO CHANGE
    b. in that
    c. where that
    d. when

26. What is the closest synonym to the underlined word?
    a. pumps
    b. streams
    c. passes
    d. courses

27. If the underlined word is grammatically incorrect, which choice is correct?
    a. NO CHANGE
    b. distinguishes
    c. is deposed of
    d. composes

28. For what purpose did the writer enclose the underlined phrase in parentheses?
    a. To make sure the reader wouldn't miss it
    b. Because the information is explanatory
    c. Because there are too many clauses in the sentence
    d. Because it changes the cadence of the sentence

29. In this sentence, one comma is missing. Which choice correctly shows where should the comma be inserted?

a. When this happens, and the conventional pathway is blocked the unconventional uveoscleral pathway takes on greater importance because uncontrolled increases in intraocular pressure can result in damage to the optic nerve, visual field loss, and even blindness.

b. When this happens and the conventional pathway is blocked the unconventional uveoscleral pathway takes on greater importance, because uncontrolled increases in intraocular pressure can result in damage to the optic nerve, visual field loss, and even blindness.

c. When this happens and the conventional pathway is blocked the unconventional uveoscleral pathway takes on greater importance because uncontrolled increases in intraocular pressure can result, in damage to the optic nerve, visual field loss, and even blindness.

d. When this happens and the conventional pathway is blocked, the unconventional uveoscleral pathway takes on greater importance because uncontrolled increases in intraocular pressure can result in damage to the optic nerve, visual field loss, and even blindness.

30. Which idea is not supported in the essay?

a. Glaucoma is a serious disease.

b. People with hypertension are more prone to developing glaucoma than people whose blood pressure is within the normal range.

c. Normally, ninety percent of aqueous fluid drains through the trabecular meshwork.

d. It could be years before symptoms of glaucoma appear.

Questions 31–45 are based on the following passage:

Wallace Stevens constructs a microcosm within his highly metaphorical, highly (31) ambiguous poem "Anecdote of the Jar." (32) He establishes authority over the poem's tiny world, proclaims himself the god and ruler of it, and then assumes responsibility for the life of his new world's reality. (33) Stevens accomplishes this in two ways: first, through the physical act of placing an object in an environment, and second, through the imaginative act of enlivening the inanimate object and (34) imbuing it with the power to subdue and order the environment into which it was placed. The poet, who in the role of speaker, ultimately controls the object in a concrete, physical sense, and who in the role of poet, (35) controls the amount of power he attributes to the object in an abstract, imaginative sense, thus deifies himself as a god-like creator through the process of inventing the fictive anecdote of the poem.

The single definitive "I" is the first word of the poem, the only identification the reader has of the nameless speaker. It summons to mind the first words of Yahweh to Moses, "I am who am," as well as God's words at the beginning of the Bible, "I am the Alpha." Stevens is a (36) Deistic type of god, setting the poem in motion by an act of creation, then narrating via his poem the events that follow without interfering in them.

The object the poet/god creates is a jar; round and tall, bare and gray. (37) He situates it on a top of a hill in the rural Tennessee wilderness. Enthroned on the hill, the jar is separate from the wilderness below; (38) this and the simple smooth shape of the jar connote the classical form of Greek temples such as the Acropolis. The wilderness is "slovenly," indicating it is primitive and uncivilized, and considered in the light of metaphorical interpretations (poet as creator, jar as temple), "slovenly" suggests the wilderness embodies unenlightened tendencies and therefore can be likened to primitive peoples.

The relationship of the jar to the landscape is one of subjugation. (39) <u>The jar commandingly "takes dominion everywhere" and demands that the wilderness produce an order it is not capable of delivering</u>. When order is not rendered, the jar attempts to tame and civilize the natural surroundings. The landscape is not, (40) <u>moreover</u>, completely reshaped and reformed by the jar. (41) <u>Although it is wild no longer, it raises and sprawls around the hill, assuming a prostrate, slavish position, yet also shows the jar that it has managed to retain a degree of its innate nature, its slovenliness.</u>

The poem dramatizes and (42) <u>paints</u> an act of creation and one of manipulation. It ends on an ambiguous note, prompting the questions, "What are the consequences for the poet?" "Does Stevens continue to believe in the microcosm he has created, even as it becomes repressive?" or "If given the chance, would he begin again and create a different world, a <u>different outcome</u>?" (43, 44, 45)

31. What is the closest synonym to the underlined word?
    a. confusing
    b. oracular
    c. equivocal
    d. definite

32. Which word or phrase could be eliminated to make the sentence less wordy?
    a. "the poem's tiny"
    b. "god and"
    c. "responsibility for"
    d. "the life of"

33. In which choice is the sentence punctuated correctly?
    a. NO CHANGE.
    b. Stevens accomplishes this in two ways, first through the physical act of placing an object in an environment and second through the imaginative act of enlivening the inanimate object and imbuing it with the power to subdue and order the environment into which it was placed.
    c. Stevens accomplishes this in two ways. First, through the physical act of placing an object in an environment, and second, through the imaginative act of enlivening the inanimate object and imbuing it with the power to subdue and order the environment into which it was placed.
    d. Stevens accomplishes this in two ways first, through the physical act of placing an object in an environment, and second, through the imaginative act of enlivening the inanimate object and imbuing it with the power to subdue and order the environment into which it was placed.

34. Which word would NOT be an acceptable substitution for the underlined word?
    a. infusing
    b. inoculating
    c. instilling
    d. inspiring

35. What is the flaw in the underlined passage?
    a. Length
    b. The words "abstract" and "imaginative" are redundant
    c. The words "deifies" and "god-like" are repetitious
    d. The word "anecdote" should be "antidote"

36. What does a Deistic god do?
    a. Creates new worlds
    b. Sets poems in action
    c. Creates a world and manages what happens in it
    d. Creates a world then sits back and watches it

37. In the underlined passage, what literary device is the author of the passage referring to?
    a. Theme
    b. Irony
    c. Setting
    d. Hyperbole

38. There is a comma missing from the underlined passage. Where does it belong?
    a. this and the simple, smooth shape of the jar connote the classical form of Greek temples such as the Acropolis
    b. this, and the simple smooth shape of the jar connote the classical form of Greek temples such as the Acropolis
    c. this and the simple smooth shape of the jar connote the classical form of Greek temples, such as the Acropolis
    d. this and the simple smooth shape, of the jar connote the classical form of Greek temples such as the Acropolis

39. How is the word "order" used in this sentence?
    a. As a noun
    b. As a verb
    c. As an adverb
    d. As an infinitive

40. Which, if any, is the correct substitution for the underlined word?
    a. NO CHANGE
    b. additionally
    c. however
    d. furthermore

41. What is the error, if any, in the underlined passage?
    a. NO CHANGE
    b. "Although" should be "Because"
    c. "wild no longer" should be "no longer wild"
    d. "raises" should be "rises"

42. The underlined word could be replaced with a word that is more appropriate. Which choice is correct?
    a. draws
    b. shows
    c. illustrates
    d. documents

43. Which question does NOT belong in the conclusion to this essay?
    a. "If the poet is satisfied, what is the quality and endurance of his poetic satisfaction?"
    b. "What is the poet's motive for giving the jar power?"
    c. "Will Stevens question why he made the microcosm as he did?"
    d. "Will Stevens wonder how the world he created reflects back upon himself, in his readers' eyes?"

44. Which metaphor is NOT appropriate for this poem?
    a. Poet as creator
    b. Jar as creator
    c. Poet as temple
    d. Wilderness as supplicant

45. Which idea is NOT supported in the essay?
    a. Poets are responsible for the types of worlds they create.
    b. Although resistant to the demands of the jar, the wilderness grudgingly obeys.
    c. Ambiguity can deepen the meaning of a poem.
    d. The wilderness is satisfied with its way of challenging the jar.

Questions 46–60 are based on the following passage:

Biscuits, the food North Americans know today as small, typically round (46) leavened and shortened breads served at meals and for snacks, have a long history, going back at least as far as the Roman Empire. The name is derived from the Latin words *bis*, which means "twice" and *coctus*, which means "cooked." (47) Loaves of plain dough (made of flour, salt, and water) were baked in an oven then sliced and left to dry (thus, twice cooked) in the oven at low heat. Because these biscuits were filling and kept well over long periods, they were a common food for sailors at sea and (48) armies on land.

Eventually beaten eggs and sugar were added to the dough and baked twice, to yield a lighter, sweeter biscuit. As spices, fruits, nuts, seeds, herbs, and cheese were mixed in, the variety of biscuits being baked at home and in factories grew abundant. (49) In the nineteenth century, the availability of cheap flour and sugar, along with chemical leavening agents such as bicarbonate of soda, led to the crusty-on-the-outside-yet-soft-on-the-inside, (50) once baked, sweet and savory biscuits of North America.

In the mid-Atlantic and southern Appalachian regions, (51) moreover, some biscuits have always been made without leavening agents. Small, dense, and hard, usually round but sometimes square, "beaten biscuits" served with ham are considered a specialty of the southern states, particularly Virginia and North Carolina. (52) Unless a kitchen was well staffed, only beaten biscuits were served when company called, generally in the afternoon with a glass of port or sherry, because of the amount of time and effort it took to prepare them. A cook would mix together an unleavened dough of flour, salt, lard, and milk or water, then beat the air out of it until the dough turned (53) smooth and glossy, and blisters formed on top. The beating was done with a wooden mallet or rolling pin on a beating board in the kitchen, or outside on a chopping block or large rock. (54) At very minimum the dough had to be whacked one hundred times but many cooks felt that was not good enough so they gave their dough from two hundred to five hundred strokes.

(55) Families who owned a beaten biscuit machine or biscuit break were fortunate indeed, as the machine broke down the dough so well it did need to be beaten. (56) Waist-high tables about

four feet long and two feet wide are topped with marble. Two stacked rollers, united by a handle (like a small clothes mangle), were located at one end and turned as the dough was fed between them. After rolling out the dough, cooks would cut it with (57) round or square metal cutters, typically painted and red with prongs embedded in the top, and then bake the biscuits until they were pale brown, yet still white inside.

Beaten biscuit machines are cherished heirlooms and museum pieces today. Modern cooks have tried to replace manual beating by running dough through meat grinders and food processors, but with modest success. Most cooks agree that it is impossible to make a true beaten biscuit without intensively beating the dough by hand. (58, 59, 60)

46. Which choice is correct?
   a. NO CHANGE
   b. levened
   c. yeasty
   d. raised

47. In this sentence, one comma is missing. Which choice correctly shows where the comma should be inserted?
   a. Loaves of plain dough, (made of flour, salt, and water) were baked in an oven then sliced and left to dry (thus, twice cooked) in the oven at low heat.
   b. Loaves of plain dough (made of flour, salt, and water) were baked in an oven then sliced and left, to dry (thus, twice cooked) in the oven at low heat.
   c. Loaves of plain dough (made of flour, salt, and water), were baked in an oven then sliced and left to dry (thus, twice cooked) in the oven at low heat.
   d. Loaves of plain dough (made of flour, salt, and water) were baked in an oven, then sliced and left to dry (thus, twice cooked) in the oven at low heat.

48. Which word would be the correct substitute for the underlined word?
   a. warriors
   b. soldiers
   c. men
   d. cavalry

49. Which part of this sentence is irrelevant to the overall meaning?
   a. "In the nineteenth century"
   b. "availability of cheap flour and sugar"
   c. "chemical leavening agents such as bicarbonate of soda"
   d. "sweet and savory"

50. If the underlined phrase is stylistically incorrect, which choice is correct?
   a. NO CHANGE
   b. baked once
   c. once-baked
   d. baked

51. If the underlined word is grammatically incorrect, which choice is correct?
    a. NO CHANGE
    b. however
    c. additionally
    d. furthermore

52. Which phrase has the word order with the clearest meaning?
    a. Unless a kitchen was well staffed, beaten biscuits were only served when company called
    b. Unless a kitchen was well staffed, only beaten biscuits were served when company called
    c. Unless a kitchen was well staffed, beaten biscuits only were served when company called
    d. Unless a kitchen was well staffed, beaten biscuits were served only when company called

53. Choose the pair of words that is the closest substitute for "smooth and glossy."
    a. "pliable and shiny"
    b. "sleek and satiny"
    c. "uniform and polished"
    d. "silken and light"

54. In this sentence, one semicolon is missing. Which choice correctly shows where the comma should be inserted?
    a. At very minimum, the dough had to be whacked one hundred times; but many cooks felt that was not good enough, so they gave their dough from two hundred to five hundred strokes.
    b. At very minimum, the dough had to be whacked; one hundred times but many cooks felt that was not good enough, so they gave their dough from two hundred to five hundred strokes.
    c. At very minimum, the dough had to be whacked one hundred times but many cooks felt that was not good enough; so they gave their dough from two hundred to five hundred strokes.
    d. At very minimum; the dough had to be whacked one hundred times but many cooks felt that was not good enough, so they gave their dough from two hundred to five hundred strokes.

55. If there is an error in this sentence, which choice corrects it?
    a. NO CHANGE
    b. Families who owned a beaten biscuit machine or biscuit-breaking machine were fortunate indeed, as the machine broke down the dough so well it did not need to be beaten.
    c. Families who owned a beaten biscuit machine or biscuit break were fortunate indeed, as the machine broke down the dough so well it did not need to be beaten.
    d. Families who owned a beaten biscuit machine or biscuit break were very fortunate, as the machine broke down the dough so well it did need to be beaten.

56. What is the error in the underlined passage?
    a. Marble was not available in the southern states.
    b. The phrase "Waist-high" should be "waist high."
    c. The word "are" should be "were."
    d. The word "about" should be "approximately."

57. Which of the details about the cutters is least important?
    a. The shape
    b. The material they were made from
    c. The color
    d. The prongs

58. What helped the variety of biscuits to grow?
    a. Bicarbonate of soda
    b. Flavorful ingredients
    c. Cheap flour and sugar
    d. Ease of preparing soft biscuits

59. Why weren't beaten biscuits served often at family meals?
    a. They were considered fancy food, for when company came calling.
    b. It was just too hot in the South to go outside and beat dough for long.
    c. They took a long time to chew because they were so hard.
    d. It took a lot of effort to whip up a batch.

60. Which idea is NOT supported in the essay?
    a. Cooks were particular about how many times they beat the dough.
    b. Biscuits were considered a staple food.
    c. Cooks beat the dough to incorporate air into it.
    d. Ancient Romans ate biscuits.

Questions 61–75 are based on the following passage:

Sir Thomas More's utopian society is based on the philosophy that society is (61) <u>better</u> than the sum of individual wills. The government's main purpose is to help its citizens thrive by providing the means to a peaceful, comfortable life. To that end, a democracy of sorts is established by the election of local officials. The society values human rights and equality over private ownership, (62) <u>but</u> rules are based on communal ownership. Communal life supplies a social structure that limits the nature and desirability of personal choice.

(63) <u>The communal society regulates the hours its citizens spend working it controls when, where, and what they eat, and dictates the amount of time they spend in recreation.</u> Utopians are not allowed to settle permanently in one location to live and work; rather, by law of the community they are compelled to work at least two years on farms in the countryside. To travel to another city, a citizen must obtain leave from the local official and stipulate exactly how many days they will be away from home.

Nothing is private in Utopia; citizens, under the watchful eyes of their neighbors, spend their time performing labor and participating in approved forms of leisure. Through constant surveillance, the community imposes order on its citizens. (64) <u>For instance, lectures are held every morning and a citizen may choose between spending that time attending a lecture or working at their trade, as it has been resolved by the community at large that they will pursue one or the other.</u> They cannot exert the personal freedom of choosing an alternative, such as staying at home and doing as they please.

As Utopia knows no wealth, no private property, and no type of luxury, the inhabitants lead (65) <u>humble and upright lives</u>, uncluttered by materialistic goals and personal ambition. (66) <u>In exchange for the freedom of individual choice the Utopian society provides plentiful food, personal safety, exceptional medical care, religious freedom, and freedom from war.</u>

(67) <u>In direct contrast, the society described in Niccolò Machiavelli's *The Prince* is structured as a hierarchy, with a prince as its (68) autocratic ruler.</u> With the aid of a body of councilors, the prince rules the common people in matters of state, rather than in matters of (69) <u>personal affairs</u>. Power

politics, a cabinet of wise advisors, and the goodwill of the people are paramount to a successful prince. A prince should be ambitious and take risks on great municipal projects, not so much to improve the quality of life for citizens, but to enhance his own glory in their eyes and thus secure his (70) reign.

Excelling at art of warfare helps a prince achieve his goals and maintain his political might. He must be able to acquire and hold new principalities, (71) quash internal insurrection, and make alliances, using whatever means at his disposal, including cruelty and duplicity, if necessary.

Citizens in Machiavelli's society exercise free self-will. They are at liberty to do whatever they please, but they know that if they are found guilty of breaking any of the prince's laws, they will suffer a penalty. In this society, most denizens desire wealth, and honest people are encouraged to toil to earn the comforts and security that riches can bring. (72) Because nothing is guaranteed by the state, life is harsher for some, and more stable for most, than in the utopian society. The prince promises neither a physically comfortable existence nor a spiritually happy one, only the latitude of personal freedom of choice for his citizens to set goals for themselves, and a political and social environment in which it is possible to achieve them. (73, 74, 75)

61. What is the best substitute for the underlined word?
    a. NO CHANGE
    b. greater
    c. stronger
    d. more powerful

62. What is the best substitute for the underlined word?
    a. NO CHANGE
    b. Thus
    c. However
    d. Interestingly

63. In this sentence, a semicolon is missing. Which choice correctly shows where the semicolon should be inserted?
    a. The communal society regulates the hours its citizens spend working it controls when, where, and what; they eat, and dictates the amount of time they spend in recreation.
    b. The communal society regulates the hours its citizens spend; working it controls when, where, and what they eat, and dictates the amount of time they spend in recreation.
    c. The communal society regulates the hours its citizens spend working it controls when, where, and what they eat; and dictates the amount of time they spend in recreation.
    d. The communal society regulates the hours its citizens spend working; it controls when, where, and what they eat, and dictates the amount of time they spend in recreation.

64. Which is the clearest way to break this sentence into two sentences?

    a. For instance, lectures are held every morning and a citizen may choose between spending that time attending a lecture or working at their trade, as it has been resolved by the community. They will pursue one or the other.

    b. For instance, lectures are held every morning a citizen may choose. Between spending that time attending a lecture or working at their trade, as it has been resolved by the community at large that they will pursue one or the other.

    c. For instance, lectures are held every morning and a citizen may choose between spending that time attending a lecture or working at their trade. It has been resolved by the community at large that citizens will pursue one or the other, lectures or work.

    d. For instance, lectures are held every morning. And a citizen may choose between spending that time attending a lecture or working at their trade, as it has been resolved by the community at large that they will pursue one or the other.

65. Choose the pair of words that is the closest substitute for "humble and upright."

    a. "self-conscious and stiff"

    b. "modest and virtuous"

    c. "lowly and tense"

    d. "self-effacing and righteous"

66. In this sentence, a comma is missing. Which choice correctly shows where the comma should be inserted?

    a. In exchange, for the freedom of individual choice the Utopian society provides plentiful food, personal safety, exceptional medical care, and religious freedom.

    b. In exchange for the freedom of individual, choice the Utopian society provides plentiful food, personal safety, exceptional medical care, and religious freedom.

    c. In exchange for the freedom of individual choice, the Utopian society provides plentiful food, personal safety, exceptional medical care, and religious freedom.

    d. In exchange for the freedom of individual choice the Utopian society provides, plentiful food, personal safety, exceptional medical care, and religious freedom.

67. What is the best way to improve the underlined passage?

    a. NO CHANGE

    b. There should be a comma after "*Prince.*"

    c. The words "prince" and "autocratic" are redundant.

    d. The word "is" should precede "structure."

68. What is the meaning of the underlined word?

    a. The ruler rules one kingdom only.

    b. The ruler has absolute power.

    c. The ruler is a tyrant.

    d. The ruler has only one counselor.

69. Which is NOT an example of "personal affairs" in a Machiavellian society?

    a. What a person eats for breakfast

    b. What time a person attends a lecture

    c. Punishment for stealing

    d. Which cities a person visits

70. What is the best substitute for the underlined word?
    a. NO CHANGE
    b. rein
    c. riegne
    d. rain

71. In the context of this essay, what is the BEST synonym for the underlined word?
    a. quell
    b. quaff
    c. squash
    d. qualm

72. Which change best improves the underlined sentence?
    a. NO CHANGE
    b. The word "nothing" should be "everything."
    c. The word "state" should be "utopian society."
    d. The word "more" should be "less."

73. Which statement about life in Utopia is FALSE?
    a. All citizens must attend a lecture or work in the morning.
    b. Travel is restricted.
    c. Citizens enjoy freedom of worship.
    d. Utopians will go to war to protect their way of life, but only if absolutely necessary.

74. Which statement about life in a Machiavellian society is FALSE?
    a. Cruelty and duplicity are strongly encouraged.
    b. Machiavellians will go to war to protect their wealth and power.
    c. Public projects are undertaken for the good of the people.
    d. Wealth can bring security.

75. Which idea is NOT supported in the essay?
    a. Utopians value community more than self-will.
    b. Wealth is distributed unevenly in a Machiavellian society.
    c. It is preferable to live in a utopian society.
    d. It is more comfortable to live in a utopian society.

Reading

Literary Narrative

The following is an excerpt from <u>Dracula</u> by Bram Stoker. Read it then answer the following ten questions.

Suddenly, away on our left, I saw a faint flickering blue flame. The driver saw it at the same moment; he at once checked the horses, and, jumping to the ground, disappeared into the darkness. I did not know what to do, the less as the howling of the wolves grew closer; but while I wondered the driver suddenly appeared again, and without a word took his seat, and we resumed our journey. I think I must have fallen asleep and kept dreaming of the incident, for it seemed to be repeated endlessly, and now looking back, it is like a sort of awful nightmare. Once the flame appeared so near the road, that even in the darkness around us I could watch the driver's motions. He went rapidly to where the blue flame arose—it must have been very faint, for it did not seem to illumine the place around it at all—and gathering a few stones, formed them into some device. Once there appeared a strange optical effect: when he stood between me and the flame he did not obstruct it, for I could see its ghostly flicker all the same. This startled me, but as the effect was only momentary, I took it that my eyes deceived me straining through the darkness. Then for a time there were no blue flames, and we sped onwards through the gloom, with the howling of the wolves around us, as though they were following in a moving circle.

At last there came a time when the driver went further afield than he had yet gone, and during his absence, the horses began to tremble worse than ever and to snort and scream with fright. I could not see any cause for it, for the howling of the wolves had ceased altogether; but just then the moon, sailing through the black clouds, appeared behind the jagged crest of a beetling, pine-clad rock, and by its light I saw around us a ring of wolves, with white teeth and lolling red tongues, with long, sinewy limbs and shaggy hair. They were a hundred times more terrible in the grim silence which held them than even when they howled. For myself, I felt a sort of paralysis of fear. It is only when a man feels himself face to face with such horrors that he can understand their true import.

All at once the wolves began to howl as though the moonlight had had some peculiar effect on them. The horses jumped about and reared, and looked helplessly round with eyes that rolled in a way painful to see; but the living ring of terror encompassed them on every side; and they had perforce to remain within it. I called to the coachman to come, for it seemed to me that our only chance was to try to break out through the ring and to aid his approach. I shouted and beat the side of the calèche, hoping by the noise to scare the wolves from that side, so as to give him a chance of reaching the trap. How he came there, I know not, but I heard his voice raised in a tone of imperious command, and looking towards the sound, saw him stand in the roadway. As he swept his long arms, as though brushing aside some impalpable obstacle, the wolves fell back and back further still. Just then a heavy cloud passed across the face of the moon, so that we were again in darkness.

When I could see again the driver was climbing into the calèche, and the wolves had disappeared. This was all so strange and uncanny that a dreadful fear came upon me, and I was afraid to speak or move. The time seemed interminable as we swept on our way, now in almost complete darkness, for the rolling clouds obscured the moon. We kept on ascending, with occasional periods of quick descent, but in the main always ascending. Suddenly, I became conscious of the fact that the driver was in the act of pulling up the horses in the courtyard of a vast ruined castle, from whose tall black windows came no ray of light, and whose broken battlements showed a jagged line against the moonlit sky.

1. The tone of this passage can be said to be:
    a. Joyful and excited
    b. Weak and Trembling
    c. Angry and solitary
    d. Terrified and desperate

2. As it is used in the first paragraph, the word *optical* most nearly means:
    a. Visual
    b. Audible
    c. Sensible
    d. Credible

3. The narrator describes the coachman's approach through the wolves:
    a. as if the coachman were going to harm the speaker.
    b. as if a supernatural phenomenon was taking place.
    c. as if it enraged the wolves instead of making them retreat.
    d. as if the speaker had had the same experience in the past.

4. What happens to the speaker after the experience with the wolves?
    a. He becomes weary and falls asleep.
    b. He gets excited and faints.
    c. He falls out of the carriage and gets eaten by wolves.
    d. He becomes so afraid he cannot speak or move.

5. Which of the following events mentioned in the passage happened first chronologically?
    a. The coach and horses were surrounded by hungry wolves.
    b. The carriage pulls up to the ruined castle.
    c. The coachman disappears into the woods after seeing a blue flame.
    d. The coachman chases the wolves away with the sweep of his hand.

6. What is the first incident that awakens the speaker's fear?
    a. When the speaker sees the blue flickering flame.
    b. When the speaker hears the wolves howling.
    c. When the ghostly coachman reappears.
    d. When the ring of wolves surrounds the speaker and carriage.

7. How does the narrator describe his experience in hindsight?
    a. Like a sort of awful nightmare.
    b. Like darkness rising all around.
    c. Like an impossible obstacle.
    d. Like a ruined castle against a moonlit sky.

8. In paragraph 3, what does the speaker compare the wolves to as in a metaphor?
    a. A cluster of teeth and saliva.
    b. A living ring of fire.
    c. A living ring of terror.
    d. A cacophony of howls.

9. As it is used in the first paragraph, the word *interminable* most nearly means:
    a. Obligatory
    b. Infinite
    c. Wretched
    d. Cumbersome

10. The speaker is describing what kind of experience in this passage?
    a. A journey to a castle.
    b. A hike in the woods.
    c. A moonlight river journey.
    d. A stormy night lost in the woods.

Social Science

Passage A

(from "Free Speech in War Time" by James Parker Hall, written in 1921, published in <u>Columbia Law Review</u>, Vol. 21 No. 6)

> In approaching this problem of interpretation, we may first put out of consideration certain obvious limitations upon the generality of all guaranties of free speech. An occasional unthinking malcontent may urge that the only meaning not fraught with danger to liberty is the literal one that no utterance may be forbidden, no matter what its intent or result; but in fact it is nowhere seriously argued by anyone whose opinion is entitled to respect that direct and intentional incitations to crime may not be forbidden by the state. If a state may properly forbid murder or robbery or treason, it may also punish those who induce or counsel the commission of such crimes. Any other view makes a mockery of the state's power to declare and punish offences. And what the state may do to prevent the incitement of serious crimes which are universally condemned, it may also do to prevent the incitement of lesser crimes, or of those in regard to the bad tendency of which public opinion is divided. That is, if the state may punish John for burning straw in an alley, it may also constitutionally punish Frank for inciting John to do it, though Frank did so by speech or writing. And if, in 1857, the United States could punish John for helping a fugitive slave to escape, it could also punish Frank for inducing John to do this, even though a large section of public opinion might applaud John and condemn the Fugitive Slave Law.

Passage B

(from "Freedom of Speech in War Time" by Zechariah Chafee, Jr. written in 1919, published in <u>Harvard Law Review</u> Vol. 32 No. 8)

The true boundary line of the First Amendment can be fixed only when Congress and the courts realize that the principle on which speech is classified as lawful or unlawful involves the balancing against each other of two very important social interests, in public safety and in the search for truth. Every reasonable attempt should be made to maintain both interests unimpaired, and the great interest in free speech should be sacrificed only when the interest in public safety is really imperiled, and not, as most men believe, when it is barely conceivable that it may be slightly affected. In war time, therefore, speech should be unrestricted by the censorship or by punishment, unless it is clearly liable to cause direct and dangerous interference with the conduct of the war.

Thus our problem of locating the boundary line of free speech is solved. It is fixed close to the point where words will give rise to unlawful acts. We cannot define the right of free speech with the precision of the Rule against Perpetuities or the Rule in Shelley's Case, because it involves national policies which are much more flexible than private property, but we can establish a workable principle of classification in this method of balancing and this broad test of certain danger. There is a similar balancing in the determination of what is "due process of law." And we can with certitude declare that the First Amendment forbids the punishment of words merely for their injurious tendencies. The history of the Amendment and the political function of free speech corroborate each other and make this conclusion plain.

11. Which one of the following questions is central to both passages?
    a. What is the interpretation of the first amendment and its limitations?
    b. Do people want absolute liberty or do they only want liberty for a certain purpose?
    c. What is the true definition of freedom of speech in a democracy?
    d. How can we find an appropriate boundary of freedom of speech during wartime?

12. The authors of the two passages would be most likely to disagree over which of the following?
    a. A man is thrown in jail due to his provocation of violence in Washington D.C. during a riot.
    b. A man is thrown in jail for stealing bread for his starving family, and the judge has mercy for him and lets him go.
    c. A man is thrown in jail for encouraging a riot against the U.S. government for the wartime tactics although no violence ensues.
    d. A man is thrown in jail because he has been caught as a German spy working within the U.S. army.

13. The relationship between Passage *A* and Passage *B* is most analogous to the relationship between the documents described in which of the following?

    a. A journal article in the Netherlands about the law of euthanasia that cites evidence to support only the act of passive euthanasia as an appropriate way to die; a journal article in the Netherlands about the law of euthanasia that cites evidence to support voluntary euthanasia in any aspect.

    b. An article detailing the effects of radiation in Fukushima; a research report describing the deaths and birth defects as a result of the hazardous waste dumped on the Somali Coast.

    c. An article that suggests that labor laws during times of war should be left up to the states; an article that showcases labor laws during the past that have been altered due to the current crisis of war.

    d. A research report arguing that the leading cause of methane emissions in the world is from agriculture practices; an article citing that the leading cause of methane emissions in the world is from the transportation of coal, oil, and natural gas.

14. The author uses the examples in the last lines of Passage *A* in order to do what?

    a. To demonstrate different types of crimes for the purpose of comparing them to see by which one the principle of freedom of speech would become objectionable.

    b. To demonstrate that anyone who incites a crime, despite the severity or magnitude of the crime, should be held accountable for that crime in some degree.

    c. To prove that the definition of "freedom of speech" is altered depending on what kind of crime is being committed.

    d. To show that some crimes are in the best interest of a nation and should not be punishable if they are proven to prevent harm to others.

15. Which of the following, if true, would most seriously undermine the claim proposed by the author in Passage *A* that if the state can punish a crime then it can punish the incitement of that crime?

    a. The idea that human beings are able and likely to change their mind between the utterance and execution of an event that may harm others.

    b. The idea that human beings will always choose what they think is right based on their cultural upbringing.

    c. The idea that the limitation of free speech by the government during wartime will protect the country from any group that causes a threat to that country's freedom.

    d. The idea that those who support freedom of speech probably have intentions of subverting the government.

16. What is the primary purpose of the second passage?

    a. To analyze the First Amendment in historical situations in order to make an analogy to the current war at hand in the nation.

    b. To demonstrate that the boundaries set during wartime are different from that when the country is at peace, and that we should change our laws accordingly.

    c. To offer the idea that during wartime, the principle of freedom of speech should be limited to that of even minor utterances in relation to a crime.

    d. To call upon the interpretation of freedom of speech to be already evident in the First Amendment and to offer a clear perimeter of the principle during war time.

17. Which of the following words, if substituted for the word *malecontent* in Passage *A*, would LEAST change the meaning of the sentence?
    a. Grievance
    b. Cacophony
    c. Anecdote
    d. Residua

18. As it is used in Passage *B*, the phrase "workable principle of classification" most nearly means:
    a. A problem to be solved.
    b. An idea able to be defined.
    c. A statement to be changed.
    d. An inquiry to be replied to.

19. What does Passage *A* say about states that forbid murder, robbery, or treason?
    a. That state is considered totalitarian and should be overturned.
    b. States that forbid murder, robbery, or treason are acting in congruence with the constitution.
    c. States that forbid murder, robbery, or treason are not acting in congruence with the constitution.
    d. That state should be able to penalize those who encourage those crimes through words.

20. What does Passage *B* say about locating the boundary line of free speech?
    a. It says that the boundary line of free speech cannot be drawn because no one can agree on a proper definition of free speech.
    b. It says that the boundary line of free speech should be drawn where any injurious statement is spoken with the purpose of harming someone.
    c. It says that the boundary line of free speech is near to the point where words spoken or in writing would give rise to illegal actions.
    d. It says that the boundary line of free speech is limitless, that there are no boundaries when it comes to speech.

Humanities

The next ten questions are from Rhetoric and Poetry in the Renaissance: A Study of Rhetorical Terms in English Renaissance Literary Criticism *by DL Clark*

To the Greeks and Romans rhetoric meant the theory of oratory. As a pedagogical mechanism it endeavored to teach students to persuade an audience. The content of rhetoric included all that the ancients had learned to be of value in persuasive public speech. It taught how to work up a case by drawing valid inferences from sound evidence, how to organize this material in the most persuasive order, how to compose in clear and harmonious sentences. Thus to the Greeks and Romans rhetoric was defined by its function of discovering means to persuasion and was taught in the schools as something that every free-born man could and should learn.

In both these respects the ancients felt that poetics, the theory of poetry, was different from rhetoric. As the critical theorists believed that the poets were inspired, they endeavored less to teach men to be poets than to point out the excellences which the poets had attained. Although these critics generally, with the exceptions of Aristotle and Eratosthenes, believed the greatest value of poetry to be in the teaching of morality, no one of them endeavored to define poetry, as they did rhetoric, by its purpose. To Aristotle, and centuries later to Plutarch, the distinguishing mark of poetry was imitation. Not until the renaissance did critics define poetry as an art of imitation endeavoring to inculcate morality . . .

The same essential difference between classical rhetoric and poetics appears in the content of classical poetics. Whereas classical rhetoric deals with speeches which might be delivered to convict or acquit a defendant in the law court, or to secure a certain action by the deliberative assembly, or to adorn an occasion, classical poetic deals with lyric, epic, and drama. It is a commonplace that classical literary critics paid little attention to the lyric. It is less frequently realized that they devoted almost as little space to discussion of metrics. By far the greater bulk of classical treatises on poetics is devoted to characterization and to the technique of plot construction, involving as it does narrative and dramatic unity and movement as distinct from logical unity and movement.

21. What does the author say about one way in which the purpose of poetry changed for later philosophers?

   a. The author says that at first, poetry was not defined by its purpose but was valued for its ability to be used to teach morality. Later, some philosophers would define poetry by its ability to instill morality. Finally, during the renaissance, poetry was believed to be an imitative art, but was not necessarily believed to instill morality in its readers.

   b. The author says that the classical understanding of poetry dealt with its ability to be used to teach morality. Later, philosophers would define poetry by its ability to imitate life. Finally, during the renaissance, poetry was believed to be an imitative art that instilled morality in its readers.

   c. The author says that at first, poetry was thought to be an imitation of reality, then later philosophers valued poetry more for its ability to instill morality.

   d. The author says that the classical understanding of poetry was that it dealt with the search for truth through its content; later, the purpose of poetry would be through its entertainment.

22. What does the author of the passage say about classical literary critics in relation to poetics?

   a. That rhetoric was more valued than poetry because rhetoric had a definitive purpose to persuade an audience, and poetry's wavering purpose made it harder for critics to teach.

   b. That although most poetry was written as lyric, epic, or drama, the critics were most focused on the techniques of lyric and epic and their performance of musicality and structure.

   c. That although most poetry was written as lyric, epic, or drama, the critics were most focused on the techniques of the epic and drama and their performance of structure and character.

   d. That the study of poetics was more pleasurable than the study of rhetoric due to its ability to assuage its audience, and the critics therefore focused on what poets did to create that effect.

23. What is the primary purpose of this passage?

   a. To contemplate the differences between classical rhetoric and poetry and to consider their purposes in a particular culture.

   b. To inform the readers of the changes in poetic critical theory throughout the years and to contrast those changes to the solidity of rhetoric.

   c. To educate the audience on rhetoric by explaining the historical implications of using rhetoric in the education system.

   d. To convince the audience that poetics is a subset of rhetoric as viewed by the Greek and Roman culture.

24. The word *inculcate* in paragraph two can be best interpreted as referring to which one of the following?
    a. Imbibe
    b. Instill
    c. Implode
    d. Inquire

25. Which of the following most closely resembles the way in which the passage is structured?
    a. The first paragraph presents us with an issue. The second paragraph offers a solution to the problem. The third paragraph summarizes the first two paragraphs.
    b. The first paragraph presents us with definitions and examples of a particular subject. The second paragraph presents a second subject in the same way. The third paragraph offers a contrast of the two subjects.
    c. The first paragraph presents an inquiry. The second paragraph explains the details of that inquiry. The last paragraph offers a solution.
    d. The first paragraph presents us with two subjects alongside definitions and examples. The second paragraph presents us with a comparison of the two subjects. The third paragraph presents us with a contrast of the two subjects.

26. Given the author's description of the content of rhetoric in the first paragraph, which one of the following is most analogous to what it taught? (The sentence is shown below.)

It taught how to work up a case by drawing valid inferences from sound evidence, how to organize this material in the most persuasive order, how to compose in clear and harmonious sentences.

    a. As a musician, they taught me that the end product of the music is everything—what I did to get there was irrelevant, whether it was my ability to read music or the reliance on my intuition to compose.
    b. As a detective, they taught me that time meant everything when dealing with a new case, that the simplest explanation is usually the right one, and that documentation is extremely important to credibility.
    c. As a writer, they taught me the most important thing about writing was consistently showing up to the page every single day, no matter where my muse was.
    d. As a football player, they taught me how to understand the logistics of the game, how my placement on the field affected the rest of the team, and how to run and throw with a mixture of finesse and strength.

27. Which of the following words, if substituted for the word *treatises* in paragraph two, would LEAST change the meaning of the sentence?
    a. Commentary
    b. Encyclopedias
    c. Sermons
    d. Anthems

28. The author mentions Aristotle in the text in order to:
    a. Persuade the audience to believe the idea that poetry is an imitative art.
    b. Portray a side of poetry that is usually ignored by the modern world.
    c. Show an exception to a common belief in the classical study of poetry.
    d. Demonstrate that poetry was not popular in the classical world.

29. The word *inculcate* in paragraph two can be best interpreted as referring to which one of the following?
   a. Destroy
   b. Mediate
   c. Outwit
   d. Impart

30. The author uses the phrase "every free-born man could and should learn" most likely to create the sense that:
   a. Learning rhetoric was extremely important to the Greeks and Romans.
   b. Free-born men were struggling to learn rhetoric in academia.
   c. The art of persuasion was not very important to the Greeks and Romans.
   d. In ancient Greece and Rome, schools did not have many resources.

Natural Science

The next ten questions are based on the following passage from The Story of Germ Life *by Herbert William Conn.*

The first and most universal change effected in milk is its souring. So universal is this phenomenon that it is generally regarded as an inevitable change which can not be avoided, and, as already pointed out, has in the past been regarded as a normal property of milk. To-day, however, the phenomenon is well understood. It is due to the action of certain of the milk bacteria upon the milk sugar which converts it into lactic acid, and this acid gives the sour taste and curdles the milk. After this acid is produced in small quantity its presence proves deleterious to the growth of the bacteria, and further bacterial growth is checked. After souring, therefore, the milk for some time does not ordinarily undergo any further changes.

Milk souring has been commonly regarded as a single phenomenon, alike in all cases. When it was first studied by bacteriologists it was thought to be due in all cases to a single species of micro-organism which was discovered to be commonly present and named Bacillus acidi lactici. This bacterium has certainly the power of souring milk rapidly, and is found to be very common in dairies in Europe. As soon as bacteriologists turned their attention more closely to the subject it was found that the spontaneous souring of milk was not always caused by the same species of bacterium. Instead of finding this Bacillus acidi lactici always present, they found that quite a number of different species of bacteria have the power of souring milk, and are found in different specimens of soured milk. The number of species of bacteria which have been found to sour milk has increased until something over a hundred are known to have this power. These different species do not affect the milk in the same way. All produce some acid, but they differ in the kind and the amount of acid, and especially in the other changes which are affected at the same time that the milk is soured, so that the resulting soured milk is quite variable. In spite of this variety, however, the most recent work tends to show that the majority of cases of spontaneous souring of milk are produced by bacteria which, though somewhat variable, probably constitute a single species, and are identical with the Bacillus acidi lactici. This species, found common in the dairies of Europe, according to recent investigations occurs in this country as well. We may say, then, that while there are many species of bacteria infesting the dairy which can sour the milk, there is one which is more common and more universally found than others, and this is the ordinary cause of milk souring.

When we study more carefully the effect upon the milk of the different species of bacteria found in the dairy, we find that there is a great variety of changes which they produce when they are allowed to grow in milk. The dairyman experiences many troubles with his milk. It sometimes curdles without becoming acid. Sometimes it becomes bitter, or acquires an unpleasant "tainted" taste, or, again, a "soapy" taste. Occasionally a dairyman finds his milk becoming slimy, instead of souring and curdling in the normal fashion. At such times, after a number of hours, the milk becomes so slimy that it can be drawn into long threads. Such an infection proves very troublesome, for many a time it persists in spite of all attempts made to remedy it. Again, in other cases the milk will turn blue, acquiring about the time it becomes sour a beautiful sky-blue colour. Or it may become red, or occasionally yellow. All of these troubles the dairyman owes to the presence in his milk of unusual species of bacteria which grow there abundantly.

31. The word *deleterious* in the first paragraph can be best interpreted as referring to which one of the following?
    a. Amicable
    b. Smoldering
    c. Luminous
    d. Ruinous

32. Which of the following best explains how the passage is organized?
    a. The author begins by presenting the effects of a phenomenon, then explains the process of this phenomenon, and then ends by giving the history of the study of this phenomenon.
    b. The author begins by explaining a process or phenomenon, then gives the history of the study of this phenomenon, this ends by presenting the effects of this phenomenon.
    c. The author begins by giving the history of the study of a certain phenomenon, then explains the process of this phenomenon, then ends by presenting the effects of this phenomenon.
    d. The author begins by giving a broad definition of a subject, then presents more specific cases of the subject, then ends by contrasting two different viewpoints on the subject.

33. What is the primary purpose of the passage?
    a. To inform the reader of the phenomenon, investigation, and consequences of milk souring.
    b. To persuade the reader that milk souring is due to Bacillus acidi lactici, found commonly in the dairies of Europe.
    c. To describe the accounts and findings of researchers studying the phenomenon of milk souring.
    d. To discount the former researchers' opinions on milk souring and bring light to new investigations.

34. What does the author say about the ordinary cause of milk souring?
    a. Milk souring is caused mostly by a species of bacteria called Bacillus acidi lactici, although former research asserted that it was caused by a variety of bacteria.
    b. The ordinary cause of milk souring is unknown to current researchers, although former researchers thought it was due to a species of bacteria called Bacillus acidi lactici.
    c. Milk souring is caused mostly by a species of bacteria identical to that of Bacillus acidi lactici, although there are a variety of other bacteria that cause milk souring as well.
    d. The ordinary cause of milk souring will sometimes curdle without becoming acidic, though sometimes it will turn colors other than white, or have strange smells or tastes.

35. The author of the passage would most likely agree most with which of the following?
    a. Milk researchers in the past have been incompetent and have sent us on a wild goose chase when determining what causes milk souring.
    b. Dairymen are considered more expert in the field of milk souring than milk researchers.
    c. The study of milk souring has improved throughout the years, as we now understand more of what causes milk souring and what happens afterward.
    d. Any type of bacteria will turn milk sour, so it's best to keep milk in an airtight container while it is being used.

36. Given the author's account of the consequences of milk souring, which of the following is most closely analogous to the author's description of what happens after milk becomes slimy?
    a. The chemical change that occurs when a firework explodes.
    b. A rainstorm that overwaters a succulent plant.
    c. Mercury inside of a thermometer that leaks out.
    d. A child who swallows flea medication.

37. What type of paragraph would most likely come after the third?
    a. A paragraph depicting the general effects of bacteria on milk.
    b. A paragraph explaining a broad history of what researchers have found in regard to milk souring.
    c. A paragraph outlining the properties of milk souring and the way in which it occurs.
    d. A paragraph showing the ways bacteria infiltrate milk and ways to avoid this infiltration.

38. In the first paragraph, what is the phenomenon that is said to be well understood?
    a. Discovery of bacteria in milk.
    b. The process of milk souring.
    c. The knowledge that sugar is converted to lactic acid.
    d. That the sour taste of milk is caused from bacteria.

39. The word *remedy* in paragraph three can be best interpreted as referring to which one of the following?
    a. Taste
    b. Apprehend
    c. Magnify
    d. Correct

40. The author mentions the dairyman in the last paragraph of the text in order to:
    a. Debunk the myth that dairymen cause milk souring themselves by leaving the lid open to spoiling.
    b. Give credit to the dairyman by showing how he is able to counteract milk souring.
    c. Add credibility to the passage by showing a practical element of the consequences of milk souring.
    d. Avoid talking about the lack of knowledge they have about milk souring by changing the subject.

Answer Explanations #2
English

1. A: The sentence is correct as written. CE is a fairly new term and stands for Common Era. Its usage is now preferred over AD, or Anno Domini, which is Latin for "year of our Lord" (the year Christ was born).

2. C: "Medieval," Choice *C*, is the correct spelling.

3. D: The word "its" is the best word to use here. "Its" shows possession, even with no apostrophe. The possession would be its (art's) moral aspects. The word "it's" shows the contraction for "it is." The word its' is not in use in the English language. "Their" is incorrect because the word "art" is a singular noun, and so it needs a singular pronoun, "its."

4. B: This question concerns itself with keeping tenses consistent. In this sentence, "Illuminated" should be "illuminates" (Choice *B*), in keeping with the present tense verb "reflects." The verb "clarifies" (Choice *D*) is in the present tense, but "clarifies" does not mean the same thing as "illuminates."

5. A: Choice *A* is correct because introductory phrase is followed by a comma. Choice *B* is incorrect because the comma separates two items of a list of two, a situation in which a comma is not needed. Choice *C* is incorrect because the comma's placement chops up the introductory phrase. Choice *D* is incorrect because the comma falls before an open parenthesis; commas can never do this.

6. D: While Choices *A*, *B*, and *C* might well describe Europe during the Dark Ages, Choice *D* ("unsettled") best addresses the void that was left when the Roman Empire fell.

7. D: In this case, the focus is the place in the world where humanity belongs. This calls for the possessive form "man's," as in Choice *D*. Choice *A* ("mans") is incorrect because it does not exist as a variant of "man." Choice *B* (mans') is plural possessive rather than singular possessive. Choice *C* (men's) is the possessive form of "men," not of "man."

8. A: Choices *B*, *C*, and *D* ("applauding," "encouraging," and "inspiring," respectively) do not come as close to matching the word "lauding" as does Choice *A* ("praising").

9. C: The commas in Choice *C* set off the prepositions "of" and "on" so that the reader does not stumble on them, and the prepositions are correctly matched to the nouns they are paired with. "Contemplation on God" in Choice *A* is grammatically incorrect, as is "meditation of God" in Choice *B*. "Contemplating and meditating on God" (Choice *D*) is a shorthand for "contemplating on," and therefore it is incorrect.

10. B: Choice *B* is correct because it further illustrates how art was used as a means of communication. Even wealthy people who knew how to read and write had little access to the written word, and no means of producing it other than by writing on paper. With no mass publications, artwork became all the more crucial for communicating to everyone, not just the poor or just the rich.

11. A: "Aesthetic" is the correct word; it is defined as "of or pertaining to the sense of the beautiful." Choice *B* ("technical") is exactly what the artists were not focusing on, technical skills and achievement. Choice *C* sounds similar to "aesthetic," but it denotes being in a state of ecstasy. And "art-worthy" (Choice *D*) is an ambiguous term.

12. B: "Infant" (Choice *A*) most closely matches "baby," although the other choices do describe Jesus.

13. C: Choice *C* is correct: "than" is needed here, not "then." There are no reasons to make the suggested changes in Choices *A*, *B*, and *D*.

14. B: Of all the choices, the phrase in Choice *B* ("—if not outright decline—") could be cut because it offers further commentary on what has already been stated, the fact that cultural stagnation had set in. Choice *A* makes the statement untrue. Choices *C* and *D* are neither parentheticals nor refinements of an idea, and therefore they should not be cut.

15. C: Choice *C* is correct. The opening thesis promises a discussion of how the Church helped preserve medieval artwork, but preservation is never further addressed in the essay. Choice *A* is incorrect, and Choices *B* and *D* appear in the essay.

16. B: The question is asking about number agreement. The subject of the verb "result" is the singular noun "group," in the prepositional phrase "group of conditions." Therefore Choice *B* is correct, because it is the correct form for a singular verb. As written (Choice *A*), the verb "result" incorrectly agrees in number with the plural noun "conditions." Choice *C* ("Glaucoma results") is grammatically correct, but it oversimplifies what glaucoma is by omitting mention of the group of conditions. Choice *D* ("Glaucoma is a condition that results") is factually inaccurate.

17. D: The underlined word is used incorrectly; the correct answer is Choice *D*, "affected." "Effected" (Choice *A*) means to produce something as a result. "Infected" (Choice *B*) is a good guess, as this is an essay about a disease, but the opening sentence defines glaucoma as a group of conditions, never mentioning infection. "Afflicted" (Choice *C*) is also a good guess, because glaucoma can certainly be viewed as an affliction, but "affected" still remains the best choice because it is more objective than "afflicted."

18. B: Although this is a fairly long sentence, it requires only one internal punctuation mark, a comma, as Choice *B* shows. The sentence begins with a long subordinate clause that starts with the subordinating conjunction "because." The structure of the sentence is: "Because X and Y, Z happens." Choice *A* is incorrect because it mistakenly groups "early stages" with the clinicians' actions. Choice *C* is incorrect because it splits the subordinate clause; it is like writing, "Because X, and Y, Z happens." Choice *D* is incorrect because the excessive use of commas makes it choppy to read.

19. B: Choice *B*, "eye care professionals," is the correct choice because it encompasses Choice *A* ("eye surgeons"), Choice *C* ("optometrists"), and Choice *D* ("ophthalmologists"), all of whom are trained to recognize the symptoms of glaucoma.

20. D: In this sentence, "however" must be replaced by the correct conjunctive adverb "although" (Choice *D*). Choice *B* is also a conjunctive adverb, joining the two main clauses while also acting as an adverb to modify the second clause, but it is a synonym of "however" and so is incorrect. Choice *C* ("but") is a coordinating conjunction and does not work in this sentence. The coordinating conjunction "and" would be acceptable in its place.

21. C: The word "anterior" comes from the Latin word *ante*, which means "before," so it is logical to conclude that the anterior chamber of the eye is the foremost one, Choice *C*.

22. D: An "alternative" pathway is, in this case, an "additional" one, so Choice *D* is correct. "Connective" does not mean "alternative," it means a joining of two separate things, so Choice *A* is incorrect. Choice *B* is incorrect; "alternative" means there is an additional pathway but does not necessarily mean the additional pathway is inferior. Choice C, "emergency" is incorrect because there is no indication that the eye uses the uveoscleral pathway for drainage in emergency situations only.

23. B: Choice B is correct because the long introductory clause ends just before "IOP might," and the introductory clause needs to be set off with a comma. In Choice A, the verb "prevents" shows incorrect noun and verb agreement with the subject "resistance," so Choice A is incorrect. In Choice C, "might" is correct because there is a chance IOP could increase; "may" indicates it is being allowed to increase. In Choice D, removing "to" is incorrect because there are two parallel phrases: "to the retina" and "to the shape of the tissue."

24. A: Choice A is correct. The essay states several times that the aqueous fluid flows *from* the anterior chamber; anterior means front, so the fluid flows from the front to the back. Therefore pressures builds up at the back. The changes suggested in Choices B, C, and D are unnecessary.

25. A: Choice A ("NO CHANGE") is correct. This construction is a preposition, "in," in front of a relative pronoun, "which," and is appropriate here. Choice B, "in that," means "for the reason that" and is not appropriate here. Choice C ("where that") is nonsensical, and Choice D ("where") is too colloquial for medical writing.

26. C: "Pumps," "streams," and "courses" (Choices A, B, and D, respectively) are all more vigorous than "flows." The correct answer is Choice C, "passes," because it is gentler.

27. A: "Comprises" is the correct usage, so Choice A is the correct answer. Choice B, "distinguishes," would change the meaning of the sentence, because it means "to recognize," so this is incorrect. Choice C, "is deposed of," does not make sense. "Composes" (Choice D) appears here as an active verb, so it is incorrect.

28. B: The writer put the phrase "labeled 'unconventional' because it is not a distinct pathway" in parentheses because the information is interesting but not totally necessary. In other words, it is explanatory, Choice B. The other choices represent secondary reasons for putting this information in parentheses.

29. D: The comma should be inserted at the end of the introductory clause, as shown in Choice D. Choice A is incorrect because the comma interrupts the introductory clause. Choice B is incorrect because the comma placement does not create two complete clauses. Choice C is incorrect because the comma insertion makes the first part of the sentence into a run-on clause and the second part distorts the writer's intended meaning.

30. B: Choice B is correct. The essay points out that people with ocular hypertension tend toward glaucoma, not people with high blood pressure. Choices A, C, and D are all stated in the essay.

31. C: Choice C, "equivocal," is the closest match to "ambiguous." Choice A, "confusing," means puzzling or baffling without the connotation of having an alternative meaning, so this is incorrect. Choice B ("oracular") pertains to being prophetic, which the poem might be to some readers, but this is not a synonym for the word "ambiguous." Choice D, definite, means something clear or *un*ambiguous, which is an antonym for the word "ambiguous."

32. D: Choice D ("the life of") could most readily be cut because "the life of his new world's reality" is a long and ungainly phrase; being responsible for "his new world's reality" is enough. Eliminating the phrase "the poem's tiny" (Choice A) eliminates necessary information about what kind of world is being discussed. Deleting the phrase "responsibility for" (Choice *C*) would mean the poet assumes the life of his poem, which he does not do.

33. A: Choice *A* is correct because the colon introduces two complex clauses that are internally punctuated and separated by a comma. Choice *B* is incorrect because the comma is not as good a choice as the colon for introducing examples. Choice *C* is incorrect because the second sentence is now a fragment. Choice *D* is incorrect because placing the comma after "first" makes it modify "accomplishes."

34. B: Choices *A*, *C*, and *D* are all fine synonyms for "imbuing." Choice *B* ("inoculating") is a medical term and therefore inappropriate.

35. C: Choice *C* is the correct answer because "deifies" and "god-like" can be construed as repetitious. The length (Choice *A*) is appropriate; "abstract" and "imaginative" are not redundant (Choice *B*); and "anecdote" and "antidote" (Choice *D*) are not interchangeable.

36. D: The answer to this question can be found through context. The writer says Stevens first creates the world of his poem and then records what happens, which is Choice *D*. In Choices *A* and *B*, he commits only one action in each sentence; in Choice *C* he creates and then manages his world.

37. C: It's important to know that the jar is on a hill in rural Tennessee wilderness, as these details describe the poem's setting. Choice *A*, theme, is the overall idea conveyed throughout the body of the poem, and this describes only one of the poem's details, so this is incorrect. Choice *B* is incorrect; irony is the expression of language in which the opposite meaning is intended, and we are not given enough information here to know if this is irony. Choice *D* is incorrect; hyperbole refers to an exaggerated statement.

38. A: Choice *A* is correct because the comma separates two coordinate adjectives. Choices *B*, *C*, and *D* all contain this error.

39. A: "Order" is a noun in this sentence.

40. C: This question pertains to choosing the correct adverb. Here the jar is attempting to tame the wilderness and the wilderness resists, which calls for an adverb of contrast rather than one of inclusion. Choice *A* ("moreover"), Choice *C* ("additionally"), and Choice *D* ("furthermore") all are inclusive. Only Choice *C* ("however") indicates contrast.

41. D: Choice *A* is incorrect because it contains the error Choice *D* identifies: "raises" should be "rises." "Because" works in opposition to "although" (Choice *B*), and it is perfectly correct to say "wild no longer" (Choice *C*).

42. D: Choices *A*, *B*, and *C* ("draws," "shows," and "illustrates," respectively) have a common flaw: they don't accurately portray what the poet does: he "documents" (Choice *D*) through words.

43. B: Choices *A*, *C*, and *D* all deal with the topic of the conclusion: the consequences (if any) facing the poet. Choice *B* concerns itself with the creative act of writing poetry, and so it is the outlier.

44. B: Choices *A*, *C*, and *D* are discussed in the essay; Choice *B* ("poet as temple") is not.

45. D: The correct answer is Choice *D* because the reader might guess how the wilderness feels but is not told how it feels. According to the essay, Choices *A*, *B*, and *C* are true.

46. A: The word "leavened" is correct as is, both in appropriateness and spelling. Choice *B* is misspelled, and Choices *C* and *D* are synonyms of the underlined word.

47. D: Choice *A* is incorrect because the comma is placed in front of a parenthesis, which should never happen. To be correct, Choice *B* would need a comma after the closed parenthesis. Choice *C* is incorrect because the comma separates the noun and the verb. Therefore Choice *D* is the correct answer.

48. B: The correct answer is Choice *B*, "soldiers," because it is parallel in usage to the preceding term, "sailors." Comparing "sailors" to "armies" is awkward because "sailors" are individuals and "armies" are groups. (Comparing "navies" to "armies" would be fine.) Choice *A*, "warriors," is technically correct, but it is too colorful to be paired with the plain word "sailors." Choice *C* is grammatically correct but less specific than "soldiers." Choice *D* is too specific, since cavalry refers to mounted troops.

49. B: The new information in this sentence is the introduction of chemical leavening agents, so Choice *B* is correct. Choices *A*, *C*, and *D* are mentioned in the sentence, but they are subordinate to Choice *B*.

50. C: In Choice *C*, the hyphen in "once-baked" makes it clear that "once-baked" modifies "biscuits." As the sentence is written, "once baked," set off by commas, could be read as a parenthetical reference to time ("the biscuits, after they are baked..."), so Choice *A* is incorrect. Choice *B* is incorrect because it's difficult to tell if "once baked" is intended as an adjective modifying the texture or modifying the biscuits. Choice *D* is not the best answer because it does not specify that the biscuits are baked only once.

51. B: This question pertains to choosing the correct adverb. The discussion is transitioning from leavened biscuits to unleavened ones, which means an adverb of contrast is needed, rather than one of inclusion. Choice *A* ("moreover"), Choice *C* ("additionally"), and Choice *D* ("furthermore") all are inclusive. Only Choice *B* ("however") indicates contrast.

52. D: This question involves proper placement of the adverb "only," which should precede the noun/verb combination it modifies. The word "only" should also be as close to the noun/verb combination as possible. Choice *D* is correct because the only time beaten biscuits were served was when company came by. Choices *A* and *B* are ambiguous: were the biscuits themselves receiving service, or were they only served when company came over? Choice *C* says that beaten biscuits were only served and nothing else was done with them (they were not broken, sold, disposed of, et cetera). This may be true, but it is not the point of the original sentence.

53. B: Choice *A* is incorrect because a surface that is smooth isn't necessarily pliable. Choice *C* is incorrect because "uniform" is not a synonym of "smooth." Choice *D* is incorrect because although "silken" and "smooth" are synonyms, "light" and "glossy" are not. Therefore the best answer is Choice *B*, "sleek and satiny."

54. A: Between main clauses, a comma is usually used with "and," "but," "or," "not," and "for," but using semicolons between clauses punctuated with commas lends clarity, as in Choice *A*. Choice *B* is incorrect because including "one hundred times" in the second clause makes it into nonsense. Choice *C* is incorrect because there are no commas in the clauses, and Choice *D* is incorrect because the first clause is a fragment.

55. C: Choice *C* is correct because the machine did the work of breaking down the dough. Choices *A* and *D* are incorrect because the word "not" is missing; both sentences say the dough "*did need* to be beaten." Choice *B* is incorrect because it changes "biscuit break" to "biscuit-breaking machine." The proper terminology is "biscuit break."

56. C: The error in the passage pertains to tense. Choice *C* correctly changes "are" to "were." Choice *A* is incorrect because marble actually was available in the United States and was used to top the tables. The hyphen in Choice *B* ("waist-high") is correct, and "about" (Choice *D*) is perfectly acceptable in this usage.

57. C: The color (Choice *C*) is less important than the shape of the cutters (Choice *A*), as square biscuits are mentioned earlier in the essay. The color is less important than their durability (which Choice *B* implies). The fact that the cutters had prongs in them (Choice *D*) is new information.

58. B: While Choices *A*, *C*, and *D* were important in helping biscuits become plentiful, they get their variety from the ingredients that cooks put into them, Choice *B*.

59. D: While Choices *A*, *B*, and *C* are true, it's the effort involved that kept beaten biscuits from being daily fare at a family's table (Choice *D*).

60. C: The essay states that the opposite of Choice *C* is true: beating the dough was the method used to extract air from it. Choices *A*, *B*, and *D* are all supported in the essay.

61. B: Choice *B* is correct because society is being compared to the sum of individual wills, and this calls for a word dealing with magnitude (size). "Stronger" (Choice *C*) and "more powerful" (Choice *D*) do not convey a sense of magnitude.

62. B: This sentence needs a word to unite the two clauses. Choice *A* provides a conjunction ("but"), which is not inclusive; neither is the adverb "however" (Choice *C*). "Interestingly" (Choice *D*) does not fit grammatically into the sentence. Choice *B* ("thus") is the correct answer.

63. D: If there is no coordinating conjunction between clauses in a sentence, a semicolon can link them together, as in Choice *D*. Choices *A*, *B*, and *C* are incorrect because the clauses on both side of the semicolon must stand alone grammatically, which is not the case with these misplaced semicolons.

64. C: Choices *A* and *D* are incorrect. Although they both make breaks that divide the sentence into two, each results in one long sentence and one abrupt one. Choice *C*, the correct answer, does a better job of creating two sentences that are balanced in length. Choice *B* is incorrect because it divides the sentence into two fragments, not two sentences.

65. B: Choice *B* ("modest and virtuous") is the correct answer. Neither of the words in Choices *A* and *C* ("self-conscious and stiff" and "lowly and tense," respectively) are true synonyms of the given words. The pair in Choice *D* ("self-effacing and righteous") is far wide of the mark.

66. C: Choice *C* is correct because the comma separates the introductory clause from the trunk of the sentence. Choice *A* is incorrect because the comma interrupts the introductory phrase. Choice *B* is incorrect because the sentence does not make sense as it is divided. Choice *D* is a bad choice: the sentence it creates is grammatically correct, but what it says is quite different from what the writer intended.

67. D: Choice *D* is correct because it supplies the word "is," which is missing from Choices *A*, *B*, and *C*.

68. B: All choices use the prefix "auto," meaning "one," but their suffixes determine their definitions. An autocrat is a ruler who has absolute or unrestricted power, as Choice *B* states. The autocrat may rule more than one kingdom (Choice *A*) and may have more than one counselor (Choice *D*). While the autocrat exercises absolute power, the autocrat is not a tyrant (Choice *C*), an absolute ruler who governs arbitrarily without constitutional restrictions and exercises power in a harsh and oppressive manner.

69. C: What a person eats for breakfast, when she attends a lecture, and which cities she visits are all examples of personal freedoms. The punishment for stealing is a civil matter, and so Choice *C* is correct.

70. A: The word is correct as presented in the sentence. "Rein" (Choice *B*) refers to a piece of riding tack; "riegne" (Choice *C*) is a made-up word; and "rain" (Choice *D*) is precipitation.

71. A: Choice *A*, "quell," is the most exact synonym for "quash" in this context. "Quaff," Choice *B*, means to drink. "Squash" (Choice *C*) is often erroneously used in place of "quash." And "qualm" (Choice *D*) denotes a sudden feeling of sickness or faintness.

72. D: Choice *A* is incorrect because the sentence does contain an error. Choice *B*, changing "nothing" to" everything," is incorrect because the sentence is about a Machiavellian state, in which nothing is guaranteed. Choice *C* is not correct because the subject is a Machiavellian state, not Utopia. Choice *D* identifies the error: in a Machiavellian society, life is harsher for some citizens, and less stable for most, when compared to life for Utopians.

73. D: The essay points out that Utopians enjoy freedom from war, and so Choice *D* is correct.

74. A: Choice *A* is the correct answer. Cruelty and duplicity exist as means to an end but are not strongly encouraged.

75. D: Choice *C* is not supported in the essay. The essay describes what each society is like and lets the reader decide which they would prefer.

Reading

1. D: The tone of this passage can be said to be terrified and desperate. We can see the terror in the passage through the word choice: "terrible," "fear," and "dreadful." We also know that the speaker was "paralyzed with fear" at one point and acted desperately to keep the wolves away. Choice *A*, joyful and excited, is far from the tone. Choice *B*, weak and trembling, is close, but the speaker shows more terror and desperation than he does weakness. Choice *C*, angry and solitary, is also close, but the speaker is not experiencing a solitude, rather a wish to be left alone by the wolves.

2. A: The word *optical* means *visual*. The word *optic* comes from the Greek word *optikos* which means *sight or seeing*. In the context of the passage, the speaker describes something he is seeing, so this would also refer back to a *visual* meaning.

3. B: The narrator describes the coachman's approach through the wolves as if a supernatural phenomenon was taking place. The coachman appears out of nowhere like a ghost. The speaker says he "swept his long arms"

4. D: After the speaker's experience with the wolves, he becomes so afraid he cannot speak or move. This is shown in the sentence: "This was all so strange and uncanny that a dreadful fear came upon me, and I was afraid to speak or move." The wolf attack plus the coachman's strangeness in making the wolves leave so suddenly were all too much for the speaker to handle.

5. C: The first thing that happens chronologically is that the coachman disappears into the woods after seeing a blue flame. Next is Choice *A*: the coach and horses are surrounded by hungry wolves. Next is Choice *D*: the coachman chases the wolves away with the sweep of his hand. Next is Choice *B*: the carriage pulls up to the ruined castle.

6. D: The first incident that awakens the speaker's fear is when the ring of wolves surrounds the speaker and carriage. This question deals with reading comprehension, and it's necessary to go back to the text to decide when the first moment of fear was. The word "fear" isn't mentioned until this scene in the second paragraph: "They were a hundred times more terrible in the grim silence which held them than even when they howled. For myself, I felt a sort of paralysis of fear."

7. A: The narrator describes his experience in hindsight as a sort of awful nightmare in the first paragraph: "I think I must have fallen asleep and kept dreaming of the incident, for it seemed to be repeated endlessly, and now looking back, it is like a sort of awful nightmare." For this question, it's important to know that *hindsight* is synonymous with the idea of *looking back*.

8. C: The speaker compares the wolves to a living ring of terror in the third paragraph: "but the living ring of terror encompassed them on every side."

9. B: The word *interminable* most nearly means *infinite*. In the passage, the speaker says: "The time seemed interminable as we swept on our way, now in almost complete darkness, for the rolling clouds obscured the moon." We can take a guess as to the meaning of the word from the context clues. If you have just been through a terrifying experience and are waiting to get out of it, the situation might seem to go on for an eternity until it is over.

10. A: The speaker is describing a journey to a castle. We see this at the conclusion of the passage, as the culminating journey has finally ended, and they come upon a ruined castle. Choice *B* is incorrect because the speaker and coachman are not hiking, but using a carriage pulled by horses. Choice *C* is incorrect because there is no river mentioned in the passage. Choice *D* is incorrect because there is no storm in the passage.

11. A: What is the interpretation of the first amendment and its limitations? This is a central question to both passages. Choice *B* is incorrect; a quote mentions this at the end of the first passage, but this question is not found in the second passage. Choice *C* is incorrect, as the passages are not concerned with the definition of freedom of speech, but how to interpret it. Choice *D* is incorrect; this is a question for the second passage but is not found in the first passage.

12. C: A man is thrown in jail for encouraging a riot against the U.S. government for the wartime tactics although no violence ensues. The authors would most likely disagree over this answer choice. The author of Passage *A* says that "If a state may properly forbid murder or robbery or treason, it may also punish those who induce or counsel the commission of such crimes." This statement tells us that the author of Passage *A* would support throwing the man in jail for encouraging a riot, although no violence ensues. The author of Passage *B* states that "And we can with certitude declare that the First Amendment forbids the punishment of words merely for their injurious tendencies." This is the best answer choice because we are clear on each author's stance in this situation. Choice *A* is tricky; the author of Passage *A* would definitely agree with this, but it's questionable whether the author of Passage *B* would agree with this. Violence does ensue at the capitol as a result of this man's provocation, and the author of Passage *B* states "speech should be unrestricted by censorship . . . unless it is clearly liable to cause direct . . . interference with the conduct of war." This answer is close, but it is not the *best* choice. Choice *B* is incorrect because we have no way of knowing what the authors' philosophies are in this situation. Choice *D* is incorrect because, again, we have no way of knowing what the authors would do in this situation, although it's assumed they would probably both agree with this.

13. A: Choice *A* is the best answer. To figure out the correct answer choice we must find out the relationship between Passage *A* and Passage *B*. Between the two passages, we have a general principle (freedom of speech) that is questioned on the basis of interpretation. In Choice *A*, we see that we have a general principle (right to die, or euthanasia) that is questioned on the basis of interpretation as well. Should euthanasia only include passive euthanasia, or euthanasia in any aspect? Choice *B* is incorrect because it does not question the interpretation of a principle, but rather describes the effects of two events that happened in the past involving contamination of radioactive substances. Choice *C* begins with a principle—that of labor laws during wartime—but in the second option, the interpretation isn't questioned. The second option looks at the historical precedent of labor laws in the past during wartime. Choice *D* is incorrect because the two texts disagree over the cause of something rather than the interpretation of it.

14. B: This is the best answer choice because the author is trying to demonstrate by the examples that anyone who incites a crime, despite the severity or magnitude of the crime, should be held accountable for that crime in some degree. Choice *A* is incorrect because the crimes mentioned are not being compared to each other, but they are being used to demonstrate a point. Choice *C* is incorrect because the author makes the same point using both of the examples and does not question the definition of freedom of speech but its ability to be limited. Choice *D* is incorrect because this sentiment goes against what the author has been arguing throughout the passage.

15. A: The idea that human beings are able and likely to change their mind between the utterance and execution of an event that may harm others. This idea most seriously undermines the claim because it brings into question the bad tendency of a crime and points out the difference between utterance and action in moral situations. Choice *B* is incorrect; this idea does not undermine the claim at hand but introduces an observation irrelevant to the claim. Choices *C* and *D* would most likely strengthen the argument's claim; or, they are at least supported by the author in Passage *A*.

16. D: To call upon the interpretation of freedom of speech to be already evident in the First Amendment and to offer a clear perimeter of the principle during war time. Choice *A* is incorrect; the passage calls upon no historical situations as precedent in this passage. Choice *B* is incorrect; we can infer that the author would not agree with this, because they state that "In war time, therefore, speech should be unrestricted . . . by punishment." Choice *C* is incorrect; this is more consistent with the main idea of the first passage.

17. A: The word that would least change the meaning of the sentence is *A*, grievance. Malcontent is a complaint or grievance, and in this context would be uttered in advocation of absolute freedom of speech. Choice *B*, cacophony, means a harsh noise; someone may express or "urge" a cacophony but it would be an awkward word in this context. Choice *C*, anecdote, is a short account of an amusing story. Since the word is a noun it fits grammatically inside the sentence, but anecdotes are usually thought out, and this word is considered "unthinking." Choice *D*, residua, means an outcome, and also does not make sense within this context.

18. B: The phrase "workable principle of truth" most nearly means *an idea able to be defined*. The word *principle* means a fundamental truth. If we have a workable truth that is able to be classified, we have an idea that is able to be defined. The text is talking about trying to define the concept of *freedom of speech* and the boundaries that apply.

19. D: The passage says that states that forbid murder, robbery, or treason, should also be able to penalize those who encourage those same crimes through words. Passage *A* is very clear about their stance on free speech. The author believes that the incitation of murder is just as egregious as the act of murder.

20. C: It says that the boundary line of free speech is near to the point where words spoken or in writing would give rise to illegal actions. This is found in the second paragraph of Passage B, right at the beginning of the paragraph. The passage mentions *finding* the boundary line in the first paragraph but doesn't state what that boundary line is until the second paragraph.

21. B: The author says that the classical understanding of poetry dealt with its ability to be used to teach morality. Later, philosophers would define poetry by its ability to imitate life. Finally, during the renaissance, poetry was believed to be an imitative art that instilled morality in its readers. The rest of the answer choices are mixed together from this explanation in the passage. Poetry was never mentioned for use in entertainment, which makes Choice *D* incorrect. Choices *A* and *C* are incorrect for mixing up the chronological order.

22. C: That although most poetry was written as lyric, epic, or drama, the critics were most focused on the techniques of the epic and drama and their performance of structure and character. This is the best answer choice as portrayed by paragraph three. Choice *A* is incorrect because nowhere in the passage does it say rhetoric was more valued than poetry, although it did seem to have a more definitive purpose than poetry. Choice *B* is incorrect; this almost mirrors Choice *A*, but the critics were *not* focused on the lyric, as the passage indicates. Choice *D* is incorrect because the passage does not mention that the study of poetics was more pleasurable than the study of rhetoric.

23. A: To contemplate the differences between classical rhetoric and poetry and to consider their purposes in a particular culture. Choice *B* is incorrect; although changes in poetics throughout the years is mentioned, this is not the main idea of the passage. Choice *C* is incorrect; although this is partly true, that rhetoric within the education system is mentioned, the subject of poetics is left out of this answer choice. Choice *D* is incorrect; the passage makes no mention of poetics being a subset of rhetoric.

24. B: The correct answer choice is Choice *B*, instill. Choice *A*, imbibe, means to drink heavily, so this choice is incorrect. Choice *C*, implode, means to collapse inward, and does not make sense in this context. Choice *D*, inquire, means to investigate. This option is better than the other options, but it is not as accurate as *instill*.

25. B: The first paragraph presents us with definitions and examples of a particular subject. The second paragraph presents a second subject in the same way. The third paragraph offers a contrast of the two subjects. In the passage, we see the first paragraph defining rhetoric and offering examples of how the Greeks and Romans taught this subject. In paragraph two we see poetics being defined along with examples of its dynamic definition. In the third paragraph, we see the contrast between rhetoric and poetry characterized through how each of these were studied in a classical context.

26. D: The best answer is Choice *D*. As a football player, they taught me how to understand the logistics of the game, how my placement on the field affected the rest of the team, and how to run and throw with a mixture of finesse and strength. The content of rhetoric in the passage . . . "taught how to work up a case by drawing valid inferences from sound evidence, how to organize this material in the most persuasive order, and how to compose in clear and harmonious sentences." What we have here is three general principles: 1) it taught me how to understand logic and reason (drawing inferences parallels to understanding the logistics of the game), 2) taught me how to understand structure and organization (organization of material parallels to organization on the field) and 3) it taught me how to make the end product beautiful (how to compose in harmonious sentences parallels to how to run with finesse and strength). Each part parallels by logic, organization, then style.

27. A: Treatises is most closely related to the word *commentary*. Choice *B* does not make sense because thesauruses and encyclopedias are not written about one single subject. Choice *C* is incorrect; sermons are usually given by religious leaders as advice or teachings. Choice *D* is incorrect; anthems are songs and do not fit within the context of this sentence.

28. C: To show an exception to a common belief in the classical study of poetry. Let's look at the surrounding context. The author is showing that most classical theorists of poetry believed that poetry was supposed to inculcate morality, but since Aristotle is such a major part of classical study, the author felt that it was necessary to share that Aristotle did not share this belief. In fact, Aristotle thought that poetry was an imitative art and not an art that was a source of creation itself, especially of morality.

29. D: The word *inculcate* can best be interpreted to refer to the word *impart*. *Inculcate* and *impart* both mean to infuse or instill something. In the case of the text, the speaker says that "Not until the renaissance did critics define poetry as an art of imitation endeavoring to inculcate morality . . ." This means that the critics of the renaissance saw poetry as instilling morality into its audience.

30. A: The author uses the phrase to create the sense that learning rhetoric was extremely important to the Greeks and Romans. To say that the study of rhetoric is something that every free-born man is expected to learn makes the idea of rhetoric seem like an absolute essential in education.

31. D: The word *deleterious* can be best interpreted as referring to the word *ruinous*. The first paragraph attempts to explain the process of milk souring, so the "acid" would probably prove "ruinous" to the growth of bacteria and cause souring. Choice *A*, *amicable*, means friendly, so this does not make sense in context. Choice *B*, *smoldering*, means to boil or simmer, so this is also incorrect. Choice *C*, luminous, has positive connotations and doesn't make sense in the context of the passage. Luminous means shining or brilliant.

32. B: The author begins by explaining a process or phenomenon, then gives the history of the study of this phenomenon, this ends by presenting the effects of this phenomenon. The author explains the process of souring in the first paragraph by informing the reader that "it is due to the action of certain of the milk bacteria upon the milk sugar which converts it into lactic acid, and this acid gives the sour taste and curdles the milk." In paragraph two, we see how the phenomenon of milk souring was viewed when it was "first studied," and then we proceed to gain insight into "recent investigations" toward the end of the paragraph. Finally, the passage ends by presenting the effects of the phenomenon of milk souring. We see the milk curdling, becoming bitter, tasting soapy, turning blue, or becoming thread-like. All of the other answer choices are incorrect.

33: A: To inform the reader of the phenomenon, investigation, and consequences of milk souring. Choice *B* is incorrect because the passage states that Bacillus acidi lacticic is not the only cause of milk souring. Choice *C* is incorrect because, although the author mentions the findings of researchers, the main purpose of the text does not seek to describe their accounts and findings, as we are not even told the names of any of the researchers. Choice *D* is tricky. We do see the author present us with new findings in contrast to the first cases studied by researchers. However, this information is only in the second paragraph, so it is not the primary purpose of the *entire passage*.

34. C: Milk souring is caused mostly by a species of bacteria identical to that of Bacillus acidi lactici although there are a variety of other bacteria that cause milk souring as well. Choice *A* is incorrect because it contradicts the assertion that the souring is still caused by a variety of bacteria. Choice *B* is incorrect because the ordinary cause of milk souring *is known* to current researchers. Choice *D* is incorrect because this names mostly the effects of milk souring, not the cause.

35. C: The study of milk souring has improved throughout the years, as we now understand more of what causes milk souring and what happens afterward. None of the choices here are explicitly stated, so we have to rely on our ability to make inferences. Choice *A* is incorrect because there is no indication from the author that milk researchers in the past have been incompetent—only that recent research has done a better job of studying the phenomenon of milk souring. Choice *B* is incorrect because the author refers to dairymen in relation to the effects of milk souring and their "troubles" surrounding milk souring and does not compare them to milk researchers. Choice *D* is incorrect because we are told in the second paragraph that only certain types of bacteria are able to sour milk. Choice *C* is the best answer choice here because although the author does not directly state that the study of milk souring has improved, we can see this might be true due to the comparison of old studies to newer studies, and the fact that the newer studies are being used as a reference in the passage.

36. A: The chemical change that occurs when a firework explodes. The author tells us that after milk becomes slimy, "it persists in spite of all attempts made to remedy it," which means the milk has gone through a chemical change. It has changed its state from milk to sour milk by changing its odor, color, and material. After a firework explodes, there is nothing one can do to change the substance of a firework back to its original form—the original substance is turned into sound and light. Choice *B* is incorrect because, although the rain overwatered the plant, it's possible that the plant is able to recover from this. Choice *C* is incorrect because although Mercury leaking out may be dangerous, the actual substance itself stays the same and does not alter into something else. Choice *D* is incorrect; this situation is not analogous to the alteration of a substance.

37. D: A paragraph showing the ways bacteria infiltrate milk and ways to avoid this infiltration. Choices *A*, *B*, and *C* are incorrect because these are already represented in the third, second, and first paragraphs. Choice *D* is the best answer because it follows a sort of problem/solution structure in writing.

38. B: The process of milk souring is the phenomenon that is said to be well understood. The other answer choices may be true, but they are not the specific "phenomenon" which the text mentions. The text said that "the phenomenon is well understood," and then goes on to describe the process of milk souring in detail.

39. D: The word *remedy* means to correct or fix something. In the third paragraph of the passage, the infection of milk is said to be hard to *remedy* or *correct* once it begins the souring process. It can no longer be brought back to its former health.

40. C: The author mentions the dairyman in the last paragraph in order to add credibility to the passage by showing a practical element of the consequences of milk souring. We see several different ways in which the dairyman struggles to cope with milk souring, and this adds a personal touch to the scientific passage. The other choices are not correct within the passage.

Writing Prompts

Directions

Write an organized, coherent essay about the idea of freedom of speech. In your essay, make sure you:

- State your own opinion on the topic and analyze the relationship between your opinion and at least one other opinion

- Develop and support your ideas with reasoning and examples

- Organize your ideas in a logical way

- Communicate your ideas efficiently in standard written English

Your opinion can be in full agreement with any of those given, in partial agreement, or completely different.

Sample Prompt #1

The true boundary line of the First Amendment can be fixed only when Congress and the courts realize that the principle on which speech is classified as lawful or unlawful involves the balancing against each other of two very important social interests, in public safety and in the search for truth. Every reasonable attempt should be made to maintain both interests unimpaired, and the great interest in free speech should be sacrificed only when the interest in public safety is really imperiled, and not, as most men believe, when it is barely conceivable that it may be slightly affected. In war time, therefore, speech should be unrestricted by the censorship or by punishment, unless it is clearly liable to cause direct and dangerous interference with the conduct of the war.

Sample Prompt #2

According to the plan of the convention, all judges who may be appointed by the United States are to hold their offices *during good behavior*, which is conformable to the most approved of the State constitutions and among the rest, to that of this State. Its propriety having been drawn into question by the adversaries of that plan, is no light symptom of the rage for objection, which disorders their imaginations and judgments. The standard of good behavior for the continuance in office of the judicial magistracy, is certainly one of the most valuable of the modern improvements in the practice of government. In a monarchy it is an excellent barrier to the despotism of the prince; in a republic it is a no less excellent barrier to the encroachments and oppressions of the representative body. And it is the best expedient which can be devised in any government, to secure a steady, upright, and impartial administration of the laws.

Greetings!

First, we would like to give a huge "thank you" for choosing us and this study guide for your ACT exam. We hope that it will lead you to success on this exam and for your years to come.

Our team has tried to make your preparations as thorough as possible by covering all of the topics you should be expected to know. In addition, our writers attempted to create practice questions identical to what you will see on the day of your actual test. We have also included many test-taking strategies to help you learn the material, maintain the knowledge, and take the test with confidence.

We strive for excellence in our products, and if you have any comments or concerns over the quality of something in this study guide, please send us an email so that we may improve.

As you continue forward in life, we would like to remain alongside you with other books and study guides in our library, such as;

ACCUPLACER: amazon.com/dp/1628455160

SAT: amazon.com/dp/1628455381

We are continually producing and updating study guides in several different subjects. If you are looking for something in particular, all of our products are available on Amazon. You may also send us an email!

Sincerely,
APEX Test Prep
info@apexprep.com

FREE

Free Study Tips DVD

In addition to the tips and content in this guide, we have created a FREE DVD with helpful study tips to further assist your exam preparation. **This FREE Study Tips DVD provides you with top-notch tips to conquer your exam and reach your goals.**

Our simple request in exchange for the strategy-packed DVD is that you email us your feedback about our study guide. We would love to hear what you thought about the guide, and we welcome any and all feedback—positive, negative, or neutral. It is our #1 goal to provide you with top quality products and customer service.

To receive your **FREE Study Tips DVD**, email freedvd@apexprep.com. Please put "FREE DVD" in the subject line and put the following in the email:

a. The name of the study guide you purchased.

b. Your rating of the study guide on a scale of 1-5, with 5 being the highest score.

c. Any thoughts or feedback about your study guide.

d. Your first and last name and your mailing address, so we know where to send your free DVD!

Thank you!

Made in the USA
Columbia, SC
10 June 2019